THE PRINCIPAL'S COMPANION

A Workbook for Future School Leaders

Second Edition

John D. Bowser
Retired Professor of Educational Administration
University of Saint Thomas
Houston, Texas

Ross Sherman
Coordinator of Educational Administration Program
The University of Texas at Tyler
Tyler, Texas

University Press of America, Inc.
Lanham • New York • London

Library of Congress Cataloging-in-Publication Data

Bowser, John D.
The principal's companion : a workbook for future school leaders/
John D. Bowser, Ross Sherman.--2nd ed.
cm.
1. School management and organization--Study and teaching--United
States--Handbooks, manuals, etc.   2. School principals--United
States--Handbooks, manuals, etc. I. Sherman, Ross. II. Title.
LB1738.5B68   1996   371.2'01'0711--dc20   96-14343 CIP

ISBN 0-7618-0338-6 (cloth: alk. ppr.)
ISBN 0-7618-0339-4 (pbk: alk. ppr.)

ABOUT THE AUTHORS

John D. Bowser, Ph.D. is a retired professor of educational administration. He is a former high school mathematics teacher and coach. He served as a superintendent of schools in Wisconsin and Texas for fifteen years, and directed a program in educational administration at the university level for fifteen years. Dr. Bowser received his doctorate from the University of Chicago, and his bachelors and masters degree from Ball State University.

Ross Sherman, Ed.D. is a graduate of the University of Houston and holds a masters and bachelors degree from Temple University. He is a former elementary teacher, assistant principal and principal. Currently he is serving as department chairman and associate professor of educational administration at The University of Texas at Tyler. Dr. Sherman regularly consults with school districts in the areas of developmental supervision and instructional improvement.

This book is dedicated to all the future Teachers of Teachers.

iii

CONTENTS

PREFACE

The problem of integrating theory into practice in the field of educational administration has been something with which professors and practitioners alike have wrestled. The concern for theory appears to rest in the domain of the professors of educational administration while most practicing school administrators view theory as an intellectual exercise which has little to offer as a solution to persistent problems faced in the field.

This problem of integrating theory and practice has been identified and illustrated by the writers in an unusual way. Both took graduate courses in school administration and received masters degrees in school administration before becoming school administrators. We read the various textbooks assigned to us, studied the multitude of theories, models, styles of leadership, and principles of management contained in those texts and discussed in classes, and passed the necessary tests by regurgitating the learned knowledge.

A few years after receiving our masters degrees we were appointed to administrative positions, one of us to an assistant principalship and then later to a principalship, and the other to a superintendency of a school district.

In the midst of occupying these positions, we both were in pursuit of our doctorate degrees. In so doing, we had the need and opportunity to reread several of the texts we had read during our masters programs. But in rereading those texts, for the first time we saw pictures on those pages. Suddenly Maslow's hierarchy of needs came alive. The Getzels-Guba model took on a new and deeper meaning. We could relate to Fayol's five functions of administration, and to Daniel Griffiths' point that decision making is central to all other administrative functions. Likewise, we could now for the first time relate many of our administrative experiences to the other theories, models, leadership styles, and principles of management contained in those same textbooks we had read just a few years before. Our administrative experiences gave life to the written word. In so doing, it not only helped us better understand the written word, but it also gave us a much better understanding of our world of practice. We now knew better why certain practices worked, and even why certain practices did not.

Now that we have served as professors of educational administration, we still see the same problem, but from a different viewpoint. The vast majority of the graduate students in our educational administration programs are classroom teachers; only a handful are in administrative positions, and those people have temporary certificates which means that they have had only a few courses in educational administration.

Therefore our students cannot easily relate theory to practice. They, like ourselves only a few years ago, read the words on the pages, study the content in the courses, and regurgitate the learned knowledge on tests. They see no pictures on the pages. They cannot attach experience to the content of the courses. So as professors, we try to put life to substance. We use examples and situations from our own experiences to try to put pictures on those pages in the texts, to give life to Herzberg's Motivation Theory, to illustrate how the four styles of leadership from Hersey and Blanchard can work, and to stress with examples the importance of leaders having the kind of vision that Bennis and Nanus discuss in *Leaders*.

We are trying to paint the pictures on the pages, to integrate theory and practice, and to assist the graduate students to see the importance of using theory to improve practice. But we have been uncertain as to our degree of success. Hence, the idea of *The Principal's Companion* was created.

This workbook is designed to be used in a variety of courses including the principalship, educational leadership, personnel administration, and practicum/internship programs, and to accompany the assigned texts. The activities are simulations of tasks typically associated with the principalship and are intended to give graduate students ample opportunities to use the knowledge learned from the textbook(s) in practical hands-on experiences. The students will have numerous opportunities to be creative, to use planning, leadership, and decision making skills and to apply various theories and models in determining and formulating responses to the tasks contained in the workbook.

This workbook is not intended to preclude opportunities for professors to paint pictures on the pages of assigned texts, but we do hope that the exercises and simulations will help students to also add their color schemes to those same pages, and to make the integration of theory and practice a beautiful work of art.

A WORD ABOUT

THE PRINCIPAL'S COMPANION

The Principal's Companion consists of five major sets of activities: 1) fourteen exercises comprise the **"Creating the School"** section, 2) ten exercises make up the **"Leading the School"** set, 3) eight exercises are found in the **"Preparing for Success"**section, 4) thirty-one **"In-basket Simulations,"** and 5) two **"Case Studies."** The activities in the five sets are sequenced to some extent whereby information needed for one exercise may be drawn from an earlier exercise, but it is still possible for the professor and students to select those activities which best complement the sequence and content of the course.

We should add that all the exercises have been used in our classes and reflect a great deal of refinement as a result of responses from students regarding the exercises, and that all simulations are actual situations which occurred in our experiences or in the experiences of teachers and administrators with whom we have worked.

We hope you find the workbook a refreshing addition to the teaching and learning process, and above all, we hope you enjoy doing the exercises and simulations.

CREATING THE SCHOOL

The first set of exercises, **"Creating the School,"** are activities that entail what a new principal to a school needs to be able to do.

A new principal must engage in an analysis of his/her school and the community it serves. This allows the principal to identify the needs of the school and to establish goals and objectives he/she hopes to accomplish.

Thus in the initial set of exercises, the student will first create his/her own hypothetical school. This will serve as the basis for engaging in activities to acquire skills in the following areas: staffing a school, interviewing prospective teachers, preparing a school budget, scheduling teachers and students, creating a discipline management program, preparing a student handbook, developing a public relations program, and conducting a school assessment. These are just some of the vital skills every aspiring and effective principal must possess.

We think you will find the exercises challenging and rewarding.

HYPOTHETICAL SCHOOL EXERCISE

Goal: To design a school that will be utilized in subsequent activities in this book.

Objective: The student will design a school.

Input:

There are a myriad of characteristics that make schools unique entities. The following is intended as a preliminary list to be used by the student. Other factors may be added to formulate the hypothetical school.

1) Select grade span for the school.
2) Determine enrollment for each grade in school.
3) Determine ethnic composition of student body.
4) Describe the curricular programs for the school: i.e. subjects to be taught, special student programs such as gifted and talented, at risk, and special education.
5) Describe the facilities needed for the curricular programs as well as for the support services such as, the media center, guidance and counseling, health services, administrative offices, etc.
6) List any special problems or concerns for the school: i.e. high absenteeism, low standardized test scores, need for new lab facilities, etc.

Activity:

Design a school including the characteristics listed above.

DEMOGRAPHIC STUDY EXERCISE

Goal: To develop information and knowledge about the demographic conditions of the school.

Objective: The student will conduct a demographic study of the school attendance zone and prepare a report on the characteristics of the school attendance area. (Use Hypothetical School Exercise as basis for developing the demographic study.)

Premises:

1) It is important for the principal of a school to know and understand the characteristics of the community in which his/her school is located and from which the students come.
2) Knowledge of the demographic information of the school community will enable the principal to develop curricular, co-curricular, and social programs which will meet the needs of the people in the community.
3) Knowledge of the demographic information should enable the principal to be aware of the human and capital resources available to the school and its programs.

Input:

Information regarding the demographics of a school community may come from a variety of sources. Several sources include:

1) U.S. Census tract information
2) Student enrollment information
3) Chamber of Commerce reports
4) Business organization information
5) Telephone companies, electric power companies, and other utility companies' reports
6) Municipal governments and planning commissions' reports
7) School and school district surveys
8) Historical societies' records and documents
9) Personal observations

3

Activity:

Conduct a demographic study of your school attendance area/community. You may wish to use your hypothetical school as a basis for conducting the study. After gathering the demographic information, write a report describing your school's attendance area. Information contained in the report should include at least the following items:

1) History of school community such as its early settlers, its early commercial developments, its early schools, and other vital historical information pertinent to the development of the school community.

2) Socioeconomic status of the population presently living in school community.

3) Ethnic make-up of population in community.

4) Age of population, occupation of working adults, family patterns, and types of housing found in school community.

5) Types of businesses and industries in the community and/or surrounding communities which may support or impact the school community and in which school community residents may work and/or patronize.

6) Other educational institutions located in the school community or are accessible to school community residents.

7) General economic climate of the school community and/or of the area in which the residents of the school community work.

8) List of human and capital resources available to the school and its programs.

STRATEGIC PLANNING MODEL EXERCISE

Goal: To develop strategic plans for the hypothetical school.

Objectives:

1) The student will write a mission statement for the school.
2) The student will write a set of Envision Statements for curriculum and instruction for the school.
3) The student will write a set of five year goals for the school.
4) The student will write a set of annual goals for the school.
5) The student will identify an instructional model for the school.
6) The student will plan a three year staff development calendar for the school.

Premises:

1) Long range planning is one of the most important administrative /leadership functions.
2) Long range planning is pervasive and affects all levels and facets of school operation including instruction, curriculum and program.
3) Long range planning should be projected in 3-5 year intervals.
4) Long range planning provides direction for staff development programs.
5) Long range planning provides a means of evaluating the effectiveness of the school program.

Input:

Strategic planning is one of the most important administrative functions. It is an attempt to project and articulate the direction the organization will pursue. All subsequent organizational activities should correlate with these strategic plans.

Activity:

Complete the following activities:

1) Write a one paragraph mission/philosophy statement for the school.

2) Write ten Envision Statements: five for curriculum and five for instruction.
Example:
a) We believe in the use of deductive and inductive models of instruction. (instruction)
b) We believe that concrete experiences and materials are the basis for understanding numbers and explaining mathematical processes. (curriculum)

3) Write a set of five year goals for your school in the areas of curriculum, instruction and program.
Example:
a) Train all teachers to use inductive and deductive teaching models. (instruction)
b) Implement a math program based on the use of manipulative materials. (curriculum)
c) Implement community service projects for all grade levels. (program)

4) Write a set of annual goals for your school from your five year goals.
Example:
a) To provide staff development on inquiry teaching model. (instruction)
b) To provide inservice for teachers in the use of base ten blocks. (curriculum)
c) To develop a list of public and private agencies that could benefit from service projects. (program)

5) List the instructional methods, principles and effective teaching practices that will comprise the school's instructional model.

Example:

a) Lesson Cycle
b) Inquiry Model
c) Bloom's Taxonomy
d) Reinforcement Theory
e) Motivation Theory
f) Learning Styles

6) Develop a three year staff development model for the school based on the envision statements, goals and instructional model. (Assume that there are five days of staff development annually.)

Example:

YEAR 1

Day	Topic (a.m.)	Topic (p.m.)
1	School Orientation	Lesson Cycle
2	Curriculum Topic	Inquiry Teaching
3	Discipline Management	Reinforcement Theory
4	District Speaker	Learning Styles
5	Curriculum Topic	Questioning Strategies

Note: There should be a correlation between the aforementioned activities. In essence, the envision statements serve as guiding principles in the development of the five year goals. The annual goals are then extracted from the five year goals. The annual goals should then serve as the basis for staff development.

PERSONNEL EXERCISE

Goal: To determine the professional staff for the hypothetical school.

Objectives:

1) The student will determine the number of teachers needed for the school as well as determine the necessary qualifications for the teachers.
2) The student will determine the number of other professional personnel (librarians, counselors, administrators, etc.) needed for the school as well as the necessary qualifications for these professionals.

Premises:

1) Student enrollment, class size, program objectives/needs, and fiscal resources are major factors in determining the number of professional staff needed in the school.
2) Qualifications of the individual teachers and other professional personnel include the proper certification, experience in teaching, knowledge of subject areas, ability to meet the needs of students plus many more as may be determined by the school administrator.

Input:

The professional staff of the school should consist of the best qualified people who can be employed within the financial resources available.

The principal should carefully determine how many teachers and other professional personnel are needed, and what qualifications each individual should have in order to build the most effective school staff. The cost of personnel represents the largest single cost item in the school's budget and the district's budget, so care must be exercised to insure only needed professional personnel are employed, and at the same time, that these professional personnel can carry-out the instructional responsibilities of the school in order to meet the goals of the school.

Activities:

1) List the number of teachers needed in the school by grade level/subject area.
2) List the number of other professional personnel needed in the school by position.
3) Specify the basic qualifications (certification, experience, and other particular needs) for the two groups of professional personnel.

INTERVIEW QUESTIONS EXERCISE

Goal: To prepare interview questions.

Objective: The student will prepare a series of interview
questions for prospective teaching candidates.

Premises:

1) The extent to which education succeeds will depend largely on the people employed and the effectiveness with which they discharge their duties.
2) The goal of personnel is to help the organization attract, retain and develop personnel to attain the organization's goals while meeting the individual's needs.
3) There is a limited supply of outstanding personnel and shortages are common in high demand areas.

Input:

One of the critical functions of school administration is the selection of qualified personnel to fill existing vacancies. Many districts employ a dual interview process where applicants are initially screened by the personnel department of the school district and then interviewed and selected by the principal often with the collaboration of the faculty of the school.

It is important that the building principal select applicants carefully. During the selection process it is incumbent upon the building principal to do the following:

1) Review the personnel needs for the school and the necessary qualifications of those positions which must be filled.
2) Check references thoroughly (call all references).
3) Check academic records (indication of work ethic).
4) Use team building to balance factors such as experience, curricular expertise and leadership ability amongst the faculty.

During the interview it is important to ask questions in the areas correlated with success as a teacher.
  1) Instruction
  2) Curriculum
  3) Discipline
  4) Work ethic
  5) Human relations
  6) Other

Examples:

  1) Pretend that I am watching your _____ class. Describe what I would see happening: What would you be doing and what would your students be doing? (instruction/curriculum)
  2) What is your philosophy for teaching _____? (curriculum)
  3) How do you shape the behavior of a difficult student who does not succeed with the management system used with the rest of the class? (discipline)
  4) A teaching team member lacks skill or commitment. What is your responsibility? (human relations)

The questions should assist in determining the qualifications of the candidates for the teaching positions.

Activities:

Design two questions for each of the categories above to ask in an interview of a prospective candidate. Also describe what information you hope to receive from the candidate in answering the question.

NEW TEACHER INDUCTION EXERCISE

Goal: To create a new teacher induction program.

Objective: The student will write an outline for a building level teacher induction program.

Premises:

1) Induction can strongly influence an employee's performance.
2) Induction can speed socialization into the organization, and thus promote organizational stability.
3) All new members to an organization suffer some degree of anxiety.
4) Socialization does not occur in a vacuum and is affected by colleagues, subordinates and superordinates.
5) People tend to adjust in similar ways.

Input:

Induction is the process of assisting an individual in adapting to an organization. Individuals new to an organization have to adapt or be socialized to a variety of subgroups within the organization. These groups include:

1) Formal Organization - Consists of the people occupying identified positions within the school district and school linked together for purposes of attaining the goals of the organization.
2) Informal Organization - Consists of people within the formal organization who are linked together through interpersonal relationships, i.e. have same set of personal values which may or may not be consistent with the values of the formal organization. The informal organization may affect the decisions of the formal organization.

Individuals new to an organization must also be aware of the expectations and values held by the constituents of the organization.

For a school, this means that administrators, teachers, and other personnel in the school must be knowledgeable about expectations and values of the parents and other patrons in the school community.

In addition, many individuals experience personal adjustments such as relocation from one school to another or the transition from college student to professional educator. With this in mind, it is incumbent upon the school district and campus to provide a systematic induction program for employees in their first year to increase the probability of successful performance in their new position.

Activity:

Create an outline for a building level teacher induction program using the following headings:

1) Date of activity
2) Activity or Topic
3) Presenter

Example:

DATE	TOPIC	PRESENTER
Prior to Opening of School	Tour of Building Teacher Handbook Review	Principal
Third Week of School	Progress Reports Report Cards	Assistant Principal Master Teacher
Fifth Week of School	Teacher Evaluation Procedures	Principal

SCHOOL BUDGET EXERCISE

Goal: To create the hypothetical school budget.

Objective: The student will create a budget for the school using a program budgeting format.

Premises:

1) The budget represents one of the most important documents used by a school district in achieving its overall educational objectives.
2) The budget is the financial articulation of the school's program.
3) The budget, once accepted, does in effect establish a ceiling for operation.
4) Only by careful planning and strict allocation of limited funds can all essential programs be properly funded.

Input:

The budget establishes the parameters of the school program. Revenue for the budget is acquired from federal, state and local sources. The three basic approaches of budget preparation include:

1) Program Budgeting - Budget preparation based on program objectives/needs without specified financial allocations.
2) Basic Allotment Per Pupil - Budget preparation for the school and/or program whereby a set figure is allotted per pupil.
3) Incremental Budgeting - Budget preparation where an across-the-board adjustment is made to the school's budget and its program budgets.

Funds typically controlled at the building level include:
1) General Budget Funds - Monies received from state and local sources to operate a school district for a fiscal year.
2) Activity Account Funds - Monies generated by building level activities by students and teachers and the accounts are

maintained at the building level.

Periodic budget printouts provide an accurate record of funds and are reported in the following areas:
1) Appropriation - Amount budgeted
2) Encumbrance - Amount set aside after a purchase order has been written to purchase an item.
3) Expenditure - Amount of money actually spent from the budget.
4) Balance - Amount budgeted minus amount encumbered minus amount expended.

It is important that the building principal establish and follow acceptable business practices in all financial transactions.

In preparing a school budget use the following information:

1) Enrollment for each grade in school (See Hypothetical School)
2) Annual goals for the school (See Strategic Planning Model)
3) Program objectives/needs for your school
4) Areas
   a) Capital Outlay
      1) Furniture
      2) Audio Visual Equipment
      3) Library Books
      4) AV kits and Software
      5) Other Mechanical Equipment
   b) Instructional (see attached sheet)
   c) Other
      1) Consultants   6) Awards
      2) Rentals   7) Printing
      3) Testing Materials   8) Postage
      4) Fees and Dues   9) Office Supplies
      5) Travel - Teachers and Administrators

Activities:
1) Use the Instructional Object Codes to prepare budget information for each program on the attached Form A.
2) Prepare a budget summary sheet using attached Form B.
3) List all of the capital outlay items to be purchased.

15

INSTRUCTIONAL OBJECT CODES

01 School Administration
02 Media Center
03 Gifted and Talented
04 Prekindergarten
05 Kindergarten
06 Reading
07 Language Arts
08 Social Studies
09 Math
10 Science
11 Foreign Language
12 Health
13 Physical Education
14 Art
15 Music/Choir
16 Band
17 Orchestra
18 Guidance and Counseling
19 Crime Prevention/Drug Education
20 Special Education
21 Special Education Support

22 Vocational Education
23 Industrial Arts
24 Business Education
25 Home Economics
26 Bilingual/ESL
27 Computer Education
28 Drama
29 Speech
30 Journalism
31 Tutorial Programs
32 Homebound

Note: Students may wish to add other program and object codes to meet the program budgeting needs of their hypothetical school.

BUDGET EXERCISE

FORM A

_____ SCHOOL DISTRICT

SCHOOL _____

YEAR _____

PROGRAM CODE _____

QUANTITY	DESCRIPTION	UNIT	PRICE	TOTAL

TOTAL _____

BUDGET EXERCISE

FORM B

BUDGET SUMMARY

_____ SCHOOL

NAME OF PROGRAM	CODE	TOTAL COST

SCHOOL BUDGET TOTAL_____

HIGH SCHOOL SCHEDULING EXERCISE

Goal: To create a schedule of classes for a small high school.

Objectives:

1) The student will determine the number of classes needed for the scheduling of a small high school.
2) The student will create a schedule given the number of classes needed and the certification areas of the teachers.

Premises:

1) Scheduling of students in courses, given the areas of certification of teachers and the types of facilities available, is always a challenging exercise.
2) Student and parent satisfaction with school can be affected by the kind of schedule the student gets, and whether the student is able to take all the courses he/she needs or wants.
3) Teacher satisfaction is also affected by the schedule in that teachers have preferences as to what courses they are asked to teach, and what times of the school day they have to teach certain courses and/or certain groups of students.
4) Scheduling may take the form of a traditional model of six or seven periods that meet daily or may incorporate alternative models such as block scheduling.
5) The class schedule is also impacted by such variables as the schedules of other schools in the district, school bus schedules, lunch schedules, co-curricular schedules, and shared teacher schedules.
6) Scheduling should begin with the highest grade first, then the next highest, etc. This assures that those students who have less time remaining in school are given the best opportunity to complete the requirements for completion of high school graduation.
7) Conflicts in the schedule will occur, i.e. students will not be able to take all classes requested because of the necessity to

19

schedule a number of classes during each period of the day. Students must be scheduled into required courses before scheduling them into electives. Students may have to be contacted and asked to select other electives if not all conflicts can be resolved through scheduling.

8) Single classes that include students from all grades such as band must be scheduled at a time which does not conflict with other single required classes.

Input:

1) A normal load for students is six classes.
2) The number of classes taught by teachers will be left to the student working on the exercise.
3) The number of minutes per class, number and length of activity periods, and number and length of lunch periods, are left to the student doing the exercise.
4) Ideas for resolving conflicts in the scheduling of classes for the high school students is left to the student doing the exercise.

Activity:

Create a schedule for a small high school given the following information:

1) Course Information
2) List of Students' Course Selections
3) Teacher Certification Areas

COURSE INFORMATION
Freshmen

Required Courses

1) English I
2) Algebra or Fundamentals of Math
3) World History
4) Physical Science
5) Physical Education (one semester)
6) Health Education (one semester)

Electives

1) Spanish I
2) Band
3) Industrial Arts
4) Home Economics

Sophomores

Required Courses

1) English II
2) Algebra or Geometry
3) United States History
4) Biology
5) Physical Education (two semesters)

Electives
1) Spanish I or II
2) Band
3) Industrial Arts
4) Home Economics
5) Business Education (Typing I)
6) Computer Education

Juniors

Required Courses

1) English III
2) Geometry or Trigonometry/Algebra

Electives

1) Spanish II
2) Band
3) Vocational Education (Woods)
4) Business Education (Typing I)
5) Business Education (Bookkeeping)
6) Chemistry
7) Art
8) Computer Education

Seniors

Required Courses

1) United States Government (one semester)
2) Economics (one semester)

Electives

1) English IV (college preparatory)
2) Trigonometry /Algebra
3) Computer Education
4) Physics
5) Band
6) Spanish II
7) Vocational Education (Metals)
8) Business Education (Typing II)
9) Business Education (Bookkeeping)
10) Art

LIST OF STUDENTS
COURSE SELECTIONS

All students must enroll in six courses

Freshmen

Students	Selections	
FA	Alg,	E2
FB	Alg,	E3
FC	Alg,	E1
FD	FOM,	E3
FE	Alg,	E2
FF	Alg,	E2
FG	Alg,	E1
FH	Alg,	E1
FI	FOM,	E3
FJ	FOM,	E3
FK	Alg,	E2
FL	FOM,	E2
FM	FOM,	E4
FN	FOM,	E4
FO	Alg,	E1
FP	FOM,	E3
FQ	Alg,	E2
FR	Alg,	E1
FS	Alg,	E1
FT	FOM,	E4
FU	Alg,	E2
FV	Alg,	E2
FW	FOM,	E4
FX	FOM,	E3
FY	Alg,	E2
FZ	FOM,	E1

Sophomores

Students	Selections	
SA	Geo,	E1 II
SB	Geo,	E1 II
SC	Alg,	E2
SD	Geo,	E5
SE	Geo,	E1 I
SF	Geo,	E2
SG	Geo,	E2
SH	Alg,	E3
SI	Geo,	E5
SJ	Geo,	E2
SK	Geo,	E6
SL	Alg,	E1 I
SM	Alg,	E3
SN	Geo,	E2
SO	Geo,	E1 II
SP	Geo,	E6
SQ	Alg,	E2
SR	Geo,	E1 I
SS	Geo,	E1 I
ST	Alg,	E3
SU	Geo,	E1 II
SV	Alg,	E4
SW	Geo,	E2
SX	Geo,	E1 II

Note: E courses are listed under electives.

Juniors

Students	Selections				
JA	T/A,	E2,	E6,	E7,	E8
JB	T/A,	E1,	E2,	E6,	E8
JC	T/A,	E3,	E4,	E7,	E8
JD	T/A,	E2,	E4,	E6,	E7
JE	T/A,	E4,	E5,	E7,	E8
JF	Geo,	E1,	E2,	E6,	E8
JG	T/A,	E4,	E5,	E7,	E8
JH	T/A,	E4,	E5,	E7,	E8
JI	T/A,	E2,	E4,	E7,	E8
JJ	Geo,	E3,	E4,	E7,	E8
JK	T/A,	E1,	E4,	E6,	E7
JL	T/A,	E4,	E5,	E6,	E8
JM	T/A,	E4,	E5,	E6,	E8
JN	T/A,	E1,	E2,	E6,	E7
JO	T/A,	E4,	E5,	E7,	E8
JP	T/A,	E4,	E5,	E6,	E8
JQ	T/A,	E2,	E5,	E7,	E8
JR	Geo,	E3,	E4,	E7,	E8
JS	T/A,	E4,	E5,	E6,	E7
JT	T/A,	E4,	E5,	E7,	E8
JU	T/A,	E1,	E2,	E6,	E8
JV	Geo,	E3,	E4,	E7,	E8
JW	Geo,	E3,	E4,	E7,	E8
JX	T/A,	E2,	E6,	E7,	E8
JY	T/A,	E4,	E5,	E6,	E8
JZ	T/A,	E4,	E5,	E6,	E7

Note: E courses are listed under electives.

Seniors

Students	Selections				
RA	E2,	E3,	E6,	E7,	E8
RB	E3,	E7,	E8,	E9,	E10
RC	E1,	E4,	E5,	E8,	E10
RD	E3,	E4,	E6,	E8,	E10
RE	E2,	E3,	E7,	E8,	E9
RF	E1,	E3,	E4,	E6,	E8
RG	E1,	E4,	E6,	E8,	E10
RH	E1,	E4,	E5,	E8,	E10
RI	E3,	E4,	E8,	E9,	E10
RJ	E3,	E4,	E8,	E9,	E10
RK	E3,	E5,	E8,	E9,	E10
RL	E1,	E4,	E6,	E8,	E9
RM	E1,	E4,	E5,	E6,	E8
RN	E2,	E3,	E7,	E8,	E9
RO	E3,	E4,	E6,	E8,	E9
RP	E1,	E4,	E8,	E9,	E10
RQ	E3,	E5,	E8,	E9,	E10
RR	E1,	E3,	E4,	E5,	E6
RS	E1,	E4,	E6,	E8,	E9
RT	E3,	E4,	E5,	E8,	E10
RU	E1,	E3,	E4,	E6,	E10

Note: E courses are listed under electives.

TEACHER CERTIFICATION AREAS

Teacher	Major/Minor
1) Amy Apple	Business Education/ Mathematics
2) Julie Ball	HomeEconomics/Physical Education
3) Jeanne Cross	English/Social Studies
4) Don Daniels	Physical Education/Science/Health Education
5) Ellen Ellison	Band
6) Fred Franklin	IndustrialArts/Vocational Education
7) George Garcia	Social Studies/Spanish
8) Harriet Hrlicka	Science/Mathematics/Computer Education

DISCIPLINE MANAGEMENT PROGRAM EXERCISE

Goal: To develop a discipline management program for the hypothetical school.

Objectives:

1) The student will develop a discipline management program consisting of:
   a) School-wide Rules
   b) Classroom Management Strategies
   c) Procedures for Disruptive Students
2) The student will write a letter to parents explaining the discipline management program for the school.

Premises:

1) The majority of students come to school with the intentions of displaying good behavior.
2) Most of the remainder of the students are easily managed using effective classroom management techniques.
3) Only a small percentage of students in the school require the application of the discipline management rules.

Input:

Time is the coin of teaching. It is a precious and limited commodity. However, classroom management is a prerequisite for an environment conducive to good instruction. The more time spent on classroom management, the less time available for instruction. Therefore, classroom management should be as efficient as possible. One way to accomplish this is to be proactive by engaging in systematic planning for discipline management.

Activities:

1) Write a discipline management plan for your school consisting of:

a) School-wide Rules
b) Classroom Management Strategies for Positive Behavior
c) Procedures for Handling Disruptive Students
2) Write a letter to the parents of the students in your school explaining your discipline management program.

Example:

ANYWHERE SCHOOL
DISCIPLINE MANAGEMENT PLAN

School-wide Rules

Students are to:
1) Be responsible for all actions.
2) Display good citizenship and courtesy at all times.
3) Respect the rights and property of others.

Classroom Management Strategies for Positive Behavior

1) Use positive reinforcement
2) Create a positive environment
3) Respect students
4) Model desired behavior.
5) Be organized
6) Be positive
8) Reward students appropriately
9) Communicate with parents
10) Involve students in activities other than passive listening

Procedures for Handling Disruptive Students

1) Ignore attention seeking behaviors
2) Make a plan with the individual student
   a) Determine the one undesirable behavior
   b) Determine a behavior you would like to see in its place
   c) Conference with the student
3) Conference with the parent
4) Refer to the principal
5) Document strategies used with student and parent

ANYWHERE SCHOOL
M. Principal

Anywhere, USA

Dear Parents

As the school begins it is a pleasure to welcome our students back to Anywhere School. The faculty of Anywhere is looking forward to providing an exciting and educationally rewarding experience for your child. It is our goal to assist each child to develop to his fullest capability. In order for us to provide this type of nurturing environment, we at Anywhere must promote a setting conducive to learning.

We endeavor to foster this condition by providing an instructional program of the highest quality. We accomplish this by administering instruction and materials at the student's appropriate level. In addition, we attempt to keep the students involved and on task utilizing motivational techniques and sound principles of learning.

It is our belief that if we provide students a quality instructional program and allow them an opportunity to discuss and work out common concerns, then most discipline problems will be averted.

Occasionally, however, a student will behave in a way which infringes on the rights of others to learn. At this point, it is the school's responsibility and right to correct the situation, so the school once again can be a productive environment for all students.

In an attempt to coordinate those efforts on a school wide level, certain student expectations have been established. They are as follows:
   * Be responsible for all actions
   * Display good citizenship and courtesy at all times
   * Respect the rights and property of others

In addition, all grade levels or departments establish certain procedures and expectations which they utilize to provide a climate which allows both students and teachers the opportunity to function effectively.

29

Creating the proper school setting is a vital necessity if a school is to provide a rewarding and stimulating educational environment for its students. With this in mind, we at Anywhere School have established what we feel is a comprehensive approach to fostering an atmosphere conducive to learning.

Sincerely,

M. Principal

ORIENTATION PACKET EXERCISE

Goal: Parents will become more knowledgeable about school goals, programs, and activities.

Objective: The student will create an orientation packet for parents.

Premises:

1) One basic premise school principals typically make is that informed parents are more likely to be supportive of school goals, programs, and activities than those who are not as well informed.
2) Supportive parents are more likely to encourage their children to do better in their academic studies as well as to become more involved in various school activities than non-supportive parents.

Instructional Input:

The initial contact that occurs with parents during registration provides an excellent opportunity for school personnel to project a positive image. In addition it allows the school personnel to communicate important information pertaining to the school program, policies and procedures.

Parents and students are formulating opinions concerning the school based on initial impressions received during the registration process. Also, this registration time may provide one of the few face to face contacts the parent will have with the school. Therefore, it is extremely important for school personnel to project a professional and positive demeanor.

In addition, this initial contact provides an opportune time to share relevant information with parents. One effective technique is to provide parents with an orientation packet to familiarize them with the school. One important item to be placed in the orientation packet would be an introductory welcome letter from the principal. This letter could explain the basic philosophy of the school as articulated in the mission statement. Other relevant information which can be disseminated at this time could include:

Elementary School Packet

a) Discipline Management Plan
b) Bus Information
c) Calendar of Activities
d) Parent Teacher Organization Application
e) Classroom Supply List
f) Lunch Information and Calendar
g) Other Pertinent Information

Secondary School Packet

a) Discipline Management Plan
b) Attendance Policies
c) Student Handbook
d) School Course Offerings and Schedule of Classes
e) Calendar of Athletic Events
f) List of Clubs and Activities Available
g) Parent Teacher Organization Application
h) Other Pertinent Information

The intent of the orientation packet is to promote a positive image of the school and to transmit important information to the parents.

Activities:

1) Write an introductory welcome letter to parents.
2) Prepare a packet of materials to be given to parents.

STUDENT HANDBOOK EXERCISE

Goal: To effectively communicate with students in the school regarding policies, regulations, procedures, and other information dealing with student life in the school.

Objectives: The student will develop an outline of topics and a basic description of each topic which may be used to formulate a student handbook.

Premise:

1) Students need to know the policies and regulations regarding student behavior while at school and while participating in student activities.
2) Students need to know the various procedures which they are expected to follow in matters dealing with such things as attendance and tardiness, textbook care, participation in clubs and organizations, and school supply purchases.
3) Students need to know other general information regarding school life such as names of school staff, class schedules, insurance programs which are available to students, bus schedules, lunch prices, etc.

Input:

The student handbook should contain information which students need to know in order to be a successful student at school and to be a good school citizen. Depending upon the age and maturity of the students, the grade levels within the school, the availability of student programs and activities, and local community conditions, the content of the student handbook should consist of relevant information written in easy-to-read language.

The format of the handbook can take several forms. Examples include:

1) An 8 1/2 x 11 stapled or bound handbook
2) A bifold stapled or bound handbook

3) A tri-fold flyer
4) A pocket folder on which is printed special student information.

Whatever format is selected, the handbook should be in attractive colors, possibly school colors. It should include the name of the school on the cover along with the address and phone number, and possibly a picture of the school mascot. If the school has a motto, this too could be printed on the cover. The contents of the handbook could include but not be limited to:

1) Welcome statement from the school principal
2) School day schedule
3) Names of administrators, teachers and secretarial staff
4) Registration procedures
5) Attendance procedures
6) Student conduct policies and regulations
7) Grading, report cards and progress reports' information
8) Names of clubs and organizations and membership requirements for them
9) Transportation information
10) School lunch information
11) Student insurance information
12) Student parking information
13) Graduation requirements
14) Academic requirements by grade
15) Support services available such as counselors and librarians.

Activities:

The student will develop an outline of topics which could be included in a student handbook for a school of his/her choice. The outline should include a brief description of each topic.

Also the student may want to do a lay-out of the handbook including specifying the format, the color scheme, and the order of the content topics.

PUBLIC RELATIONS PROGRAM EXERCISE

Goal: To create a public relations program for the hypothetical school.

Objective: The student will plan a public relations campaign for the hypothetical school.

Premises:

1) Public relations can be defined as activities and strategies designed to promote the school's image.
2) These activities occur:
   a) Within the community
   b) Between schools in the district and other districts
   c) Within the school, involving the faculty and students
3) Every activity or strategy has a public relations value on a scale of 1-10 and must be analyzed based on the following factors:
   a) Time required
   b) Resources required (monetary and human)
   c) Benefits to the organization

Input:

A systematic public relations program will enable the institution to accomplish its objectives and promote a positive perception of the organization. Factors which must be considered in developing a program include the grade level of the school and unique environmental features which exist, such as the socioeconomic level of the patrons, degree of multiculturism and student mobility. Finally, it's the responsibility of the building administrators, teachers, paraprofessionals and special school groups such as the parent-teacher's organization and booster groups to promote the positive image of the school through written correspondence, meetings and activities.

Activity: On the following sheet, plan a public relations program for the year.

SCHEDULE OF PUBLIC RELATIONS ACTIVITIES

Monthly Strategies - activities that reoccur each month:

September

October

November

December

January

February

March

April

May

June

July

August

SPECIAL EDUCATION EXERCISE

Goal: To develop an understanding of the legal requirements and educational needs for serving children with disabilities.

Objective: The student will conduct a study of the procedures and programs utilized in serving children with disabilities and analyze the role of the principal in insuring such procedures and programs are effective in meeting the educational needs of the children.

Premises:

1) The intent of special education is to provide free and appropriate educational services to children identified as possessing a disability.
2) Students should be placed in the least restrictive environment where they can be successful.

Instructional Input:

Special education is governed by a variety of federal and state laws, regulations, rules, case law and hearing officer decisions. Perhaps the two most significant federal legislative acts are Section 504 of the Rehabilitation Act (1973) which provided for the rights of all handicapped people and Public Law 101-476 (1991) which is the Individuals with Disabilities Act (IDEA).

IDEA defines children with disabilities as children with: mental retardation, hearing impairment including deafness, speech or language impairment, visual impairment including blindness, serious emotional disturbance, orthopedic impairments, autism, traumatic brain injury, other health impairments, or specific learning disabilities. (*See Figure 1*)

Students are identified through a child centered process consisting of referral and assessment. The referral process is designed to collect data which may include but is not limited to the following:

38

Figure 1

SPECIAL EDUCATION TERMS PRIMER

Mental Retardation
Are students who are functioning two or more standard deviations below the mean on individually administered scales of verbal, nonverbal or performance ability.

Emotional Disturbance
Are students whose emotional condition is psychologically or psychiatrically determined to adversely affects a child's educational performance.

Physical Disabilities
Are students whose body function or members are so impaired from any cause that it adversely affects a child's educational performance. (orthopedically or other health impaired)

Multiple Disabilities
Are students who meet the eligibility criteria for two or more handicapping conditions and the disabilities severely impair performance in the following areas: psychomotor, self-care, communication, social and emotional and cognition.

Visually Impairment
Are students whose sight, after medical intervention and/or other corrective procedures, is so impaired that adversely affects a child's educational performance.

Auditory Impairment
Are students whose hearing is impaired in processing linguistic information through hearing, with or without amplification, that adversely affects a child's educational performance.

Speech Impairment
Are students whose speech is so impaired and results in one of the following: stuttering, impaired articulation, language impairment, or

voice impairment that adversely affects a child's educational performance.

Learning Disabilities
Are students who are diagnosed as having a disorder in one or more of the psychological processes involved in understanding or using spoken or written language. A significant discrepancy (one standard deviation or more) exists between intellectual ability and academic achievement.

Deaf/Blind
Are students who have a combination of severe hearing and visual loss and meet criteria for Auditorial Impairment and Visual Impairment.

Autistic
Are students whose disturbance of speech and language, relatedness, perception, developmental rate and mobility adversely affects a child's educational performance.

Traumatic Brain Injury
Are students whose brain injury is caused by an external physical force that results in total or partial functional disability or psychosocial impairment that adversely affects a child's educational performance.

1) Current educational status - grades, achievement test scores, attendance, etc.
2) Recent vision and hearing screening results
3) Updated general health inventory
4) Previous educational programs such as compensatory education in which the student may have been placed
5) Parental and family history

Gathering the information for this component is the responsibility of the regular education personnel.

The second component of the child centered process is the assessment phase. The intent of the assessment process is to determine:

1) Presence of a physical, mental or emotional disability
2) Presence or absence of a significant educational need
3) Identification of specific learning competencies

The assessment includes investigation into the following areas:

1) language
2) intellectual
3) academic/developmental
4) physical
5) emotional/behavioral
6) sociological

Once the assessment phase is completed all decisions regarding the eligibility, placement and programming are determined by the Admission, Review and Dismissal (ARD) Committee. The ARD committee consists of a representative of administration, instruction, and assessment when considering assessment information. Additionally, the participants must represent general education and special education. The parent must receive notification and be invited to attend but may decide not to participate.

If the ARD committee recommends special education services for the student, then the committee is charged with creating an individual educational plan (IEP) for the student. The IEP consists of the following components:

1) A statement of the student's present competencies
2) A statement of special education and related services needed for the student
3) Annual goals to be achieved by the student
4) Short term instructional goals

The placement of students in special education is dependent upon where the individualized educational plan can best be successfully implemented. Currently many school districts are restructuring their special education programs by incorporating more inclusionary practices. In essence special education students are placed in the regular classroom and special educators provide classroom assistance as needed for these students. This technique allows special education students to have more contact with non special education students. The proposed benefits of this model include increases in student achievement and student self-concept. The key concept is to provide services to students in the least restrictive environment. In essence, when appropriate, students with disabilities should:

1) Remain in the regular education program with special education support services
2) Be educated with students who are not disabled
3) Be provided opportunities to participate in school activities on the same basis as non-disabled students
4) Be placed in a program as close as possible to student's home
5) Be offered an opportunity for interaction with non-disabled students on a regular basis

Thus, the intent of special education is to provide free and appropriate educational services to children identified as possessing a disability.

Activity:

1) Interview the person in charge of special education in your district and ask the district perspective questions listed below.
2) Interview the building principal and ask the building level perspective questions below.

42

Special Education Interview

District Perspective:

1) What is the philosophy of the district for servicing students with special needs?
2) What programs (services) exist in the district for students with special needs?
3) What personnel are available in the district to provide special education services?
4) What problems exist at the district level in providing services to students with special needs?

Building Perspective:

1) What programs exist at the building level for servicing students with special needs?
2) What personnel are available at the building to provide special education services?
3) What problems exist at the building level in providing services to special education students?

Reference

Individuals with Disabilities Education Act. (1991). 20 U.S.C. Chapter 33.

SCHOOL ASSESSMENT EXERCISE

Goal: To examine the various ways of evaluating the effectiveness of a school.

Objective: The student will create an assessment instrument to evaluate the quality of the school.

Premises:

1) Quantitative measures (test scores, drop out rates) typically are used in performance based accountability systems to measure quality.
2) Qualitative measures (surveys, observations) can provide valuable data in determining quality.
3) A comprehensive assessment would utilize both quantitative and qualitative measures.

Input:

How do you measure quality? One method is to use a performance based accountability model that utilizes quantitative measures. Quantitative measures are referred to as hard data because they yield objective statistical information. Indicators that might be used in such a system could include:

1) test scores (norm and criterion referenced)
2) graduation rates
3) drop out rates
4) student attendance
5) SAT/ACT scores
6) number of National Merit Scholars
7) other

School districts and schools can set goals and objectives based on these quantitative indicators and then measure their effectiveness in attaining those goals.

44

Another form of data that can be collected to measure the effectiveness of schools is qualitative in nature. Qualitative measures are referred to as soft data because they rely on people's perceptions or opinions. Qualitative measures might include surveys of students (*See Figure 2*), parents (*See Figure 3*) or teachers.

A comprehensive system of assessment would include both quantitative and qualitative measures.

Activity:

1) Determine a list of qualitative measures that you would use to measure the effectiveness of your school.
2) Determine a list of quantitative measures that you would use to measure the effectiveness of your school.
3) Create a survey to measure the perceptions of parents or students or teachers regarding the effectiveness of the school.

Figure 2

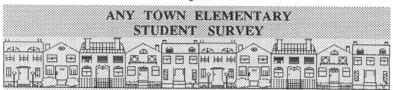

ANY TOWN ELEMENTARY
STUDENT SURVEY

The purpose of these questions is to help our school in learning more about itself. Your feelings are important. Please place a check (✓) in the space of your choice.

This is not a test. There are no right or wrong answers. We want to know how you feel. Thanks for helping.

	Yes	No	No Opinion		Yes	No	No Opinion
1. I like my school.				14. Other students are respectful of my property.			
2. Teachers seem to care about me.				15. I feel I can get help from the counselor at my school.			
3. I am proud of the work I do at school.				16. The classes at school give me a lot of chances to learn.			
4. Teachers treat me fairly.				17. I am made to feel like a good person in this school.			
5. I look forward to coming to school.				18. Students in my school are allowed to make a lot of decisions for themselves.			
6. School work is interesting to me.							
7. I like my teacher(s).				19. I usually try to do my best in school.			
8. I like to talk to my teacher(s).				20. Most adults in this school are friendly toward me.			
9. When I have a problem, I can get help from my teacher(s).				21. Students are well-behaved in my school.			
10. Punishments are given fairly at my school.				22. I feel I learn a lot at my school.			
11. Most teachers and support staff are courteous to their students at Any Town.				23. I have a lot of friends at school.			
12. Students in my school get along well together.				24. I feel I can get help at school from my principal.			
13. The things I learn at school are important to me.				25. Students have a say in what goes on in my school.			

Thank you for filling out our student survey. Please list any additional comments you may have on the back.

Figure 3

ANY TOWN ELEMENTARY
PARENT SURVEY

The purpose of this survey is to help your child's school in learning more about itself by measuring your feelings toward its program and related matters. Return to your child's teacher or the office. Surveys may also be mailed to P.O. Box 555, Any Town, Texas 75555, Attn: Any Town Elementary. Please place a check (√) in the space of your choice.

	Yes	No	No Opinion		Yes	No	No Opinion
1. I feel welcome in the school my child attends.				11. I have had at least one meaningful contact with my child's teacher(s) this year.			
2. My child's individual needs are being met in his/her school.				12. The principal of my child's school appears to be doing a good job.			
3. I am satisfied with the quality of teaching at my child's school.				13. I am given the opportunity to participate in my child's school.			
4. My child's report card gives me the kind of information I want.				14. My child usually likes to go to school.			
5. I feel free to contact the teacher(s) of my child if I have a question or problem.				15. My child's school appears to be well-stocked with learning material and equipment.			
6. I feel that I am adequately informed about the progress of my child.				16. My child is receiving an education that will help him/her become a good citizen.			
7. My child is treated fairly at school.				17. My child's teacher(s) take a personal interest in him/her.			
8. I feel there is good discipline at my child's school.				18. Services provided by the counseling staff at my child's school are adequate.			
9. My child's school keeps me adequately informed about school news.				19. My child feels his/her teacher(s) really care about him/her.			
10. I am satisfied with the organization of my child's school.				20. The school appears to be doing a good job in teaching the basic skills (math, language arts, reading).			

Your feelings are important. Thank you for filling out our parent survey. Please list additional comments on the back.

47

LEADING THE SCHOOL EXERCISES

The second set of exercises focuses on leadership. The activities are designed to assist the student to better understand the role of the principal and the leadership style(s) of the principal.

The exercises are an attempt to familiarize the student with the leadership role of the principal. Activities in this section include: interviewing a principal in order to learn more about the principalship, determining the key communicators in a school community, finding the power structure in the school community, developing a site-based decision making plan, saving a school based on the effective schools research, developing a plan for restructuring and improving the schools, and responding to three ethical situations.

Mastering the exercises and the skills in this set will prepare the student for a leadership role as a school principal and may mean the difference between being just another principal and being a truly outstanding principal.

PRINCIPAL INTERVIEW EXERCISE

Goal: To become knowledgeable about the principalship.

Objective: The student will conduct a personal interview with a principal.

Premises:

1) The principalship is a very complex position entailing a variety of functions and responsibilities.
2) Teachers tend to have a limited perception of the role of the principal.

Input:

One can not fully comprehend the principalship, its problems, its pressures, its rewards, and its potential until one is appointed to a principal's position in a school, and he/she goes into the school, goes into the principal's office and sits in the chair. Then suddenly, the weight of the position seems to lower itself on the person.

So what can a person do to learn as much about the principalship as possible, short of sitting in the chair. First, a person can observe the behavior of principals, both those who are considered effective as well as those who are not considered effective. One can learn what to do as well as what not to do.

Second a person can talk to principals, ask them questions about their job, and analyze their answers, particularly in context of the behaviors that one observes in the principals.

Third, one can become a student of the principalship. Observe principals, talk to them, but also read professional journals and books about the principalship. Learn what the position entails, its functions, duties, and responsibilities, and its problems as well as its rewards.

Activity:

1) Select a principal to interview.
2) Utilize the following questions as a guide to conduct the interview.
   a) Describe your educational background and job experiences. What did you do to prepare for this position?
   b) Describe your current position. What are the duties, functions, and responsibilities? How much time do you spend on instruction? managerial duties? student discipline?
   c) What are the most rewarding aspects of your position?
   d) What are the most stressful aspects of your position?
   e) What are the attributes needed for success as a principal?
   f) What suggestions can you provide for me as I prepare for an administrative position?
3) Summarize your overall perceptions of the interview.

LEADERSHIP STYLES EXERCISE

Goal: To identify examples of the four styles of leadership
             as described in a situational leadership model.

Objective: The student will observe and identify leadership
             behaviors of a school principal which would be
             examples of the four styles of leadership as described
             in *Leadership and the One Minute Manager*.

Premises:

1) Different situations may require different leadership styles.
2) Subordinates may have quite different and diverse
   developmental levels in their ability to work in a given
   school; in other words, some may lack enthusiasm and may
   not be very competent while others are very competent and
   highly committed to their profession.
3) The leader must have the ability to identify the developmental
   level of the subordinates, and thus utilize the appropriate
   leadership styles for the particular person or group.
4) The effectiveness of the leader is a function of the ability to
   match the appropriate leadership style to the developmental
   level of the person or group.

Input:

In *Leadership and the One Minute Manager*, Kenneth Blanchard, Patricia
Zigarmi, and Drea Zigmari discuss four leadership styles which may be
utilized by managers in their working relationships with subordinates.
The leadership styles presented by the authors in the book are in context
of the situational leadership approach Blanchard and Paul Hersey
developed in *Management of Organizational Behavior: Utilizing Human
Resources* and Hersey discussed in *The Situational Leader*.

The authors discuss how the leader must adapt his/her leadership style
to the particular needs of the subordinates. These needs are a function
of the developmental levels of the subordinates. The developmental
level, or as Blanchard and Hersey refer to it in the book *Management of*

51

Organizational Behavior: Utilizing Human Resources as "Follower Readiness," is based upon the subordinates' ability to set high but attainable goals, the ability to take responsibility, and the level of experience and education the person or group possess.

A brief description of the four leadership styles found in *Leadership and the One Minute Manager* is as follows:

THE FOUR BASIC LEADERSHIP STYLES

Style 1: Directing
The leader provides specific instructions and closely supervises task accomplishment.

Style 2: Coaching
The leader continues to direct and closely supervise task accomplishment, but also explains decisions, solicits suggestions, and supports progress.

Style 3: Supporting
The leader facilitates and supports subordinates' efforts toward task accomplishment and shares responsibility for decision making with them.

Styles 4: Delegating
The leader turns over responsibility for decision making and problem solving to subordinates.

Activities:

1) Obtain a copy of *Leadership and the One Minute Manager* (1985) and read the story regarding the four leadership styles.
2) Observe the leadership behavior of your principal at different occasions, and identify examples of his/her behavior which could be described within one of the four leadership styles found in *Leadership and the One Minute Manager*. Give at least one example per leadership style if possible.
3) Write-up the examples of the leadership styles utilized by your principal and the situations within which the examples occurred.

References

Blanchard, K., Zigarmi, P. and Zigarmi, D. (1985). *Leadership and the one minute manager*. New York: William Morrow and Company.

Hersey, P. and Blanchard, K. (1988). *Management of organizational behavior*. Englewood Cliffs: Prentice Hall.

Hersey, P. (1984). *The situational leader*. New York: Warner Books Inc.

MANAGEMENT OF TIME EXERCISE

Goal: To analyze the use of time by the principal of a school.

Objective: The student will conduct an analysis of the allocation of time which a principal of a school gives to various daily activities.

Premises:

1) The principal rarely has enough time to effectively administer a school.
2) The principal must set priorities in deciding what he/she will do in conducting the daily activities of a school.
3) How the principal sets his/her time priorities will determine what kind of principal he/she will be; that is, will the principal be an instructional leader or will the principal spend more time performing building managerial tasks.

Input:

The educational reform movement is calling for the principal to be the instructional leader of the school. This demand means that the principal must spend time in curriculum development, staff development, developmental supervision, and in general, working to improve the teaching/learning climate in the school. Instructional leadership implies that the principal must spend time working with teachers in planning and developing classroom learning activities, in observing and assisting teachers in the classroom, in assisting the teachers in evaluating the learning outcomes, and in evaluating the overall effectiveness of the teachers.

This is a new role for most principals. Many are unprepared for the role of instructional leader. But to many of the principals, it may not be a matter of expertise or desire, it is a matter of time, or in actuality, a lack of time.

Research and experience tell us that principals spend the majority of

54

their time doing managerial tasks. These tasks range from handling routine disciplinary cases, supervising custodial and maintenance personnel, handling the school budgeting and accounting matters, scheduling personnel and students, preparing correspondence, answering telephone calls, and attending meetings.

These are tasks that have to be done by somebody on the school staff, but the decision on the part of the principal may have to be, does he/she do it, or can someone else do it.

Also it must be acknowledged that the principal must perform activities that are both instructional leadership in nature as well as managerial in nature. But again, the principal must decide how much of his/her time will be devoted to instructional leadership, and how much time will be for managerial tasks. Will it be a 50-50 distribution; 70-30 in favor of instructional leadership; or what? The principal must answer that question if he/she is going to set time priorities in order to provide effective leadership for the staff as they pursue the goals of the school.

Two basic approaches may be used to determine what a principal does with his/her time. One is to ask the principal to keep a log of activities the principal does during a "typical" day and to record the amount of time devoted to each activity. In fact, it may be desirable for the principal to keep a log during different days over a two or three week period so that a better picture can evolve as to how much time the principal devotes to his/her various activities.

The second approach is for an observer to accompany the principal during one of his/her "typical" days, keeping a log of activities the principal performs and the amount of time devoted to each. This approach of observing the principal is of course time-consuming for the observer and may be difficult to do in many circumstances. But it is a technique that may prove valuable to the observer as he/she gets the opportunity to really see and experience what the principal does on a "typical" day. (Both authors recognize that principals do not have "typical" days - every day is different!)

Whatever approach is used still produces information which can be analyzed as to what the principal is doing in a day and how much time is devoted to the various activities.

Activity:

Analyze the time allocation a principal gives to various activities during a "typical" day. Ask your principal to keep a log of activities for one day and to record the amount of time devoted to each activity; or if possible, spend a day with the principal as an observer while keeping the log yourself and recording the activities and time given to each activity. The analysis can take several forms.

1) Discuss with the principal what he/she did during the day, how much time was devoted to each activity, but most importantly, how much time did the principal _desire_ to devote to each activity. Are there significant differences between the actual time the principal devoted to each of the activities and the desired time the principal indicated?

2) Classify the time allocations in percentages into the following categories:

   a) Curriculum development (planning with teachers and curriculum specialists, etc.)

   b) Improvement of instruction (visiting classrooms, assisting teachers, leading staff development, etc.)

   c) Student discipline (preparing policies, conferences with students and parents, etc.)

   d) Student activities (attending meetings, supervising restrooms, lunchrooms, bus areas, parking lots, etc., supervising co-curricular and after school student activities, etc.)

   e) Professional personnel matters (hiring, assigning, supervising, evaluating)

   f) Classified personnel matters (hiring, assigning, supervising, evaluating)

   g) School management matters (preparing correspondence, handling phone calls, preparing reports, ordering supplies, requesting maintenance, monitoring student attendance, etc.)

   h) Community activities (attending meetings in school and in the community, participating in civic groups, etc.)

3) Classify the time allocation in percentages into the following categories:
   a) One-to-one face-to-face personal encounters
   b) Small group meetings and encounters
   c) Large group meetings
   d) Telephone calls
   e) No interaction with people
4) Take the same information and classify in percentages as follows:
   a) Time in office with people
   b) Time in office alone
   c) Time in-school interacting with people
   d) Time in-school not interacting with people
   e) Time out-of-school interacting with people on school matters
   f) Time out-of-school not interacting with people on school matters
5) Classify the time in percentages if possible as to whom the principal interacted:
   a) Teachers, individually and in groups
   b) Assistant principal(s), counselor(s) and other professional support personnel in school
   c) Secretarial and other office clerical staff
   d) Custodians, maintenance personnel, and food service personnel
   e) Students - individually
   f) Students - small group
   g) Students - large group
   h) Central office personnel (Superintendent, etc.)
   i) Other district professional personnel
   j) Professional personnel out-of-district
   k) Parents
   l) Other people in community
   m) Others
6) From the above analyses, draw any conclusions or generalizations as to how your principal allocates his/her time during a typical day.

DEVELOPING THE KEY
COMMUNICATOR NETWORK EXERCISE

Goal: To develop a network of key communicators for your school community.

Objectives:

1) The student will determine those individuals within the school community who can serve as responsible key communicators for the principal and the school.
2) The student will develop ways to have two-way communications with the designated key communicators which will effectively benefit the principal, the school, and the school community.

Premises:

1) The primary purpose of the key communicator network is to improve communications between the school and community.
2) Key communicators are those people within the school community who talk to a large number of people within the community and whose ideas and opinions are respected and trusted by others from the school community.
3) Key communicators are defined as those people who are informed about the school programs and activities, who also know what the patrons of the school community are thinking, and who can get the patrons interested and/or involved in school affairs.

Input:

Key communicators are important people for a principal of a school. The key communicators can disseminate valuable information to school patrons, can squelch erroneous information and rumors found in the school community, and can communicate important information from patrons to the school principal. These key communicators are gatekeepers of information between the school and community.

58

Some of the key people to seek as possible key communicators are officers of the PTA/PTO or a school advisory group, parent volunteers, members of local civic groups and churches, local business people such as veterinarians, beauticians and barbers, coffee shop managers, local level political office holders and municipal employees, and even local school employees such as bus drivers, cafeteria workers, clerical personnel, and custodians who may reside in the school community.

The number of people who make-up the network will vary depending upon size of the community and school, the ability of the principal to work with such groups, and the availability of effective key communicators within the school community.

Contacting the individuals to invite them to serve as key communicators can be done by letter or phone, but the best way is through a personal visit in order to fully explain the purpose of the key communicator network. After affirmative responses have been received from the invited individuals, a meeting can be scheduled to further explain the purpose of the key communicator network and to disseminate information about the school and its programs. Also it is the first opportunity for the key communicators to ask questions. In any case, it can be a golden opportunity to establish good, effective communications between the school and community for the first time.

Depending upon the nature of the community and school, the key communicator group can decide how often it wishes to meet with the principal. For some school years, two meetings a year may be sufficient. At other times, if there is a lot of change or controversy in the community and in the school district and/or school, monthly meetings may be necessary.

Remember the purpose of the group is to improve the two-way communication between the school and community so as to better inform the school patrons and to improve the educational programs in the school; therefore, it is important to meet as often as necessary to meet that objective.

At the same time, the number of meetings should not be a function of the number of school crises which have arisen, but instead the number of meetings should be a function of need to disseminate information to the key communicators <u>before</u> crises arise.

Most of the contacts between the principal and the key communicators will probably be informal contacts such as telephone calls and personal visits.

Activities:

1) List several people who could be invited to be key communicators for the principal by analyzing the persons living within the school community. Indicate the qualifications and reasons for the selection of such persons.
2) List a set of activities which could be utilized to develop effective two-way communications between the school principal and the key communicators. Indicate resources needed to develop these activities and any time schedules which may pertain to the activities.

FIND THE POWER STRUCTURE EXERCISE

Goal: To define the political power structure of the school community.

Objectives: The student will conduct an analysis of the school community to determine the individuals and groups who comprise the political power structure in the school community.

Premises:

1) Every school community has individuals and groups who exercise political pressure in some manner in order to influence the decision making process within a school. In these cases the individuals/groups have vested interests in making sure that school decisions are made in accordance with their beliefs and values.

2) Some of the individuals and groups may be easily identified such as one or two officers of the PTA/PTO or even the entire governing board of the PTA/PTO. Others may not be as easily identified; they may be individuals and/or groups who work "behind-the-scenes" possibly influencing the PTA/PTO officers, school board members, or even the school staff members. These "behind-the-scenes" people may be in the same bridge club, garden club, civic organization, or church as the PTA/PTO officers, school board members, or school staff.

3) Some of the political pressure will be applied to the school principal directly in order to influence the decision making process. Other political pressures may come indirectly; that is, the political pressure will be applied to someone or to some group who may be recognized as having influence with the principal in hopes that the person or group can exercise influence on the decision making process.

4) The power individuals and groups may change over time depending upon whether the individuals and members of the groups have children in the school affected by a given decision, whether the issue or program in the school is

61

important to the individuals/groups or whether it is in conflict with the interests of the individual/groups.

5) Remember: the political power individuals and groups are in each community, so the principal must identify them and learn how to work with them.

Input:

Knowing the people or the groups who are in positions to exercise influence over what happens in your school is extremely important. Many of the individuals/groups will have the best interest of the education of the children in the school at heart. Others may not be anti-education, but the political pressures are applied to protect special interests. Those personal interests can range from making sure that the children of the individuals get the "right" teacher to insuring that a business connection with the school is maintained.

Identifying the power structure in the school community does not mean that the principal automatically assumes an adversarial position with the individuals or groups, but it does provide the principal with the basis for working with the people to plan and implement good, sound educational programs in the school, and to have the support of the political power structure while doing so.

Activity:

Conduct an analysis of the school community to determine the names of the individuals and groups who comprise the political power structure of the school community. The analysis could include but not be limited to:

1) Observing who are active members of the PTA/PTO.
2) Observing who are social friends of the PTA/PTO officers, school board members, or school staff members.
3) Noting who calls the principal or visits the principal at school to discuss various school matters.
4) Noting who may be calling the superintendent of schools or other district administrators to discuss matters pertaining to your school.

SITE-BASED DECISION MAKING EXERCISE

Goal: To demonstrate knowledge of site-based decision making as an approach for improving the school educational program.

Objectives:

The student will develop a site-based decision making (SBDM) plan for empowering staff and the community in improving the educational program of a school.

Premises:

1) Much of school administration involves making decisions about educational plans and programs.
2) Some decisions must be made by the principal solely and without time or the need to collect input from others. An example includes emergency situations which must be handled quickly.
3) Many decisions should include people who are involved in the school program and who have an vested interest in the education of students in the school. Empowerment of staff and community patrons in the decision making process gains commitment to the plans and programs for the school.
4) Site-based decision making is a process for decentralizing decisions to improve the educational outcomes of the school. Rather than have decisions made at the district level, top-down, many decisions involving personnel, programs, and problems can be and should be made at the campus level through a collaborative effort of the principal, campus staff, parents, and community patrons.

Input:

Site-based decision making (SBDM) is not a new concept, but proponents of SBDM view the recent models as very different from past efforts. Previous attempts at decentralization placed responsibility and accountability for decisions at the school board level rather than at the

63

state level. More recent efforts target individual schools. The distinction lies in whether the school is the focal point for decision making or whether decisions are sent top-down.

Recent SBDM models are based on certain assumptions:

1) The individual school is the basic decision making unit.
2) Decisions should be made at the lowest level possible.
3) The ability and expertise for educational program improvement exists with campus personnel.
4) Successful change will require full participation of those involved in the educational process.

Given these assumptions, the SBDM models emphasize shared or participatory decision making involving the principal, teachers, students, parents, and other community representatives.

Activities:

1) Develop a Site-Based Decision Making plan. Consider the following questions:
   a) What decision areas are open to shared decision making?
   b) How will the decisions be made?
   c) Who will be involved; to what degree? How will members be selected?
   d) Will there be one team or many?
   e) How will the district support the concept? What roles will district personnel play in the campus SBDM?
   f) What parameters, expectations, or limitations are involved in implementing SBDM?
2) Prepare a time schedule for the implementation of the SBDM plan.
3) Describe the desired outcomes of the Site-Based Decision Making Plan for your school.

ETHICAL DILEMMAS EXERCISE

Goal: To develop a basis for making decisions on difficult ethical questions.

Objectives: The student will react to four ethical situations using the "Ethics Check" questions.

Premises:

1) Administrators daily face ethical questions as they work with school personnel, students, parents, school salespeople and others.
2) How to respond to these ethical questions is not easy, and the basis for making decisions regarding the ethical questions tugs at the values and principles of each administrator.

Input:

Kenneth Blanchard and Norman Vincent Peale in their book *The Power of Ethical Management* develop an ethics check for individuals who must make decisions both in their professional as well as in their personal lives.

The "Ethics Check" Questions are as follows:

> The "Ethics Check" Questions

1) Is it legal?
   Will I be violating either civil law or company policy?
2) Is it balanced?
   Is it fair to all concerned in the short term as well as the long term? Does it promote win-win relationships?
3) How will it make me feel about myself?
   Will it make me proud?
   Would I feel good if my decision was published in the newspaper?
   Would I feel good if my family knew about it?

65

School principals face difficult problems every day, and many of those problems are ethical situations where one's personal and professional values and principles are subject to testing and even questioning.

In most ethical situations, there is no clear cut right and wrong answer. There exists a great deal of ambiguity within which a decision maker must find his/her position. Answering the three questions as suggested by Blanchard and Peale greatly assists one in finding an ethical solution to those difficult situations.

Activity:

Four ethical situations follow for which the student can apply the "Ethics Check" Questions, and attempt to make a decision regarding each situation.

1) The sales representative for a textbook company whose books are up for state adoption invites you as a member of the School District's textbook adoption committee to a reception at which drinks and hors d'oeures are served. Should you attend?

2) The school photographer says he will give your school a higher percentage of the sales of pictures to students if his company can retain the business with you. In the past, he has done an excellent job and the parents are pleased. But you know other photographers will charge the students less for their pictures. How do you handle this?

3) You are the supervising appraiser for a female teacher who is supporting two small children. The teacher has received merit pay. But after your scheduled classroom observation, you determine that your tentative appraisal score will not allow her to maintain her merit pay status according to local board policy. At the same time you know you could award some points on the teacher's final evaluation before your conference with her and/or award some more points through additional classroom visits. You know for the teacher to not receive the merit pay money is going to cause personal financial hardship. What do you do?

66

4) You have a teaching vacancy in your school. You have received several applications. One applicant has been recommended to you by the school board president, a leading businessman in the community. He tells you that the applicant needs to relocate in that the applicant is coming off a divorce and her former husband is a teacher in her school. The board president says the applicant is a long-time friend from their high school days in another community. You check the references of the applicant and you find both from telephone conversations with her supervisors and from written recommendations that the applicant has been a "very average teacher." You have several other applicants who have outstanding recommendations from their supervisors. What should you do ?

Reference

Blanchard, K. and Peale, N. (1988). *The power of ethical management.* New York: Fawcett Crest.

SCHOOL BOARD MEETING EXERCISE

Goal: To become familiar with the operation of a board of education.

Objective: The student will attend and report on a local school board meeting.

Premises:

1) Education is a state function locally administered.
2) The local school board is charged by the state legislature with overseeing the governance and operation of the school board.

Input:

The concept of lay control of schools was established in colonial times. Furthermore, the fact that education was not addressed in the United States Constitution meant that it fell under the reserved powers clause of the 10th amendment which reserves all powers not specifically mentioned in the Constitution for the states. Thus, education is a state function that falls under the jurisdiction of the state constitution.

In all states, the legislature has plenary power to enact laws that govern education in the state. The legislature determines functions such as:

1) financing of education.
2) determining accreditation standards.
3) establishing curriculum
4) determining powers of the local school boards
5) establishing attendance, graduation and promotion guidelines
6) determining teacher certification requirements
7) identifying state department of education responsibilities

All states except Wisconsin have a state board of education in whom the legislature delegates the responsibility to oversee education. The state board of education is charged with adopting and enforcing policies, rules and regulations that govern education in the state.

All states have a chief state school officer and in those states with a state board of education, the chief state school officer serves as the chief administrator for the department of education and professional advisor for the state board of education.

The legislature delegates the administration of local school districts to the local board of education (board of trustees). School boards typically vary in number between 5-9 members and may either be elected or appointed. Terms typically run between 2-6 years. The board is a creature of the state and is empowered with powers such as the ability to:

1) employ professional personnel
2) contract for property and services
3) set budgets and establish tax rates
4) determine curriculum, instructional methods, and instructional materials

The board's primary role is to set policy and direction for the school district.

Activity:

1) Attend a local school board meeting.
2) Secure an agenda for the meeting.
   a) What are the major sections of the agenda?
   b) What are the action items? (items to be voted on)
   c) Keep a tally of the votes on each item.
   d) Is there time for an executive (closed) session? For what purposes?
3) Note the physical arrangements and logistics.
   a) Where and when does the board meet?
   b) Diagram and describe the room and the seating of the board members, superintendent and others.
   c) How are minutes recorded?
   d) How many people are in attendance?
4) Note the interactions between board members, administrative staff and patrons.
   a) What is the superintendent's role? Board president's?
   b) Are there any patrons who address the board? If so, on

what topics? At what point on the agenda?

c) How would you characterize the interaction of board members during the discussion items?

d) Are there any voting blocks which are evident?

5) Closure - What are your general impressions of the meeting?

EFFECTIVE SCHOOLS EXERCISE

Goal: To become familiar with effective schools research.

Objective: The student will use the effective schools research to create a written response for improving the educational quality at a school identified as at risk.

Premises:

1) Some schools are more effective then others in raising the achievement levels of students, given a statistical comparison of the students.
2) Researchers of effective schools work under the premise that all students can learn. Furthermore the researcher assumes that there are differences between effective schools and less effective schools in providing a teaching/learning environment for all students to learn.

Instructional Input:

The effective schools research is a body of knowledge accumulated over the past twenty years concerning the factors that have been identified as being associated with schools that are effectively promoting student achievement. The effective schools research is broadly divided into four categories: leadership, instruction, environment and program.

The principal's leadership is a key to effective schools. Characteristics identified as being associated with effective principals include:

1) assume an assertive instructional role (Edmonds, 1979; Brookover and Lezotte, 1979)
2) provide a vision of excellence that is translated into goals and objectives (Rutherford, 1985)
3) monitor classrooms frequently (Rutherford, 1985)
4) intervene in a supportive manner (Rutherford, 1985)
5) convey high expectations for students and staff (Rutter, 1979)

The second category consists of those elements of effective schools that relate to the instructional personnel. Effective teachers display the following characteristics:

1) allot time equally among students (Fischer et al, 1980)
2) plan for smooth transitions between activities (Brophy, 1983; Billups, 1984)
3) state rules and procedures (Rutter, 1979)
4) utilize behavior modification techniques effectively (Brophy, 1983)
5) project a vision of excellence (Cahn, 1982)
6) believe in their own efficacy (Brophy, 1979)
7) make students accountable for their own learning (Rosenshine, 1983)
8) communicate and teach to an objective (Rosenshine, 1979)
9) demand and provide opportunities for achievement (Farrar et al, 1984)
10) believe students can reach their potential (Purkey and Smith, 1982; Good and Brophy, 1980)
11) exhibit objectivity (Billups, 1979)
12) use active listening (Good, 1975)
13) use a student centered style (Good, 1975; Schneider, 1981)
14) innovate with a zest for learning (Schneider, 1981)

The third category is environment. Characteristics identified as promoting an environment conducive to academic achievement include:

1) high academic emphasis (Brookover and Lezotte, 1979; Rutter, 1979)
2) orderly school environment (Edmonds, 1979)
3) parental involvement in student learning (Brookover and Lezotte, 1979)
4) maximum time on task with success (Walberg, 1988)
5) well kept school plant (Edmonds, 1979)

The final category contains those characteristics associated with the overall program. They include the following principles:

1) high academic emphasis (Rutter, 1979)
2) systematic assessment and monitoring of student progress

(Edmonds, 1979; Rutter, 1979)
3) emphasis on basic skills (Brookover and Lezotte, 1979)
4) meaningful homework assigned (Rutter, 1979)
5) regular inservice for staff (Smith and Purkey, 1982)
6) lessons adjusted to student needs (Rutter, 1979)
7) management of instructional time (Brophy, 1983; Berliner, 1984)
8) effective grouping for instruction (Brophy, 1979; Rosenshine, 1983)

It should be noted that the effective schools research has come under scrutiny concerning the nature of the research, validity of the conclusions, and the impetus it is providing for educational reform. The preponderance of the research on effective schools is correlational in nature due to the inability of the researcher to manipulate the variables under study. The second concern involves the validity of the conclusions being drawn. Stedman (1987) challenges the findings of some of the more notable studies by suggesting the findings and recommendations are not substantiated by the research and that in some instances the findings are in direct contradiction to the accepted effective schools research. Prince (1995) found a complete absence of any relationship between implementing the correlates and increases in student achievement.

Finally there is concern that the effective schools research is serving as a driving force in educational policy to mandate a narrowing of the curriculum with an undue emphasis on basic skills, uniform curriculum, and standardized testing for accountability. (Resnick and Resnick, 1985) In addition, it may be having a negative impact on low income, urban schools by focusing the curriculum on lower order test items to the exclusion of the high tech problem solving curriculum. (Meier, 1984)

Activity :

1) Read the scenario below.
2) Use the Effective Schools Research to formulate a written response to rectify the existing situation.

Can This School Be Saved ?

You are assuming the principalship of a 600 pupil school. (You may choose the grade levels) The students come from low to middle socioeconomic families, about 40% are minority, and a sizable percentage move in and out of the school during the year.

There are 40 teachers and specialists on the staff. Most of the teachers have several years of experience. However, you detect a negative attitude on the part of the teachers in that they feel that most students in the school cannot learn. As you walk through the classrooms, you observe lots of wasted time, use of paper and pencil activities, usage of a single textbook, and very few motivational techniques. Students seem bored and uninterested in their studies.

A check of the standardized test scores indicates that your school is in the lower 35 percentile of all schools. There exists a considerable discrepancy between white and minority student performance. Furthermore a review of the special populations indicates that a disproportionately high rate of minorities are in special education.

If you believe your school can make a difference in the academic progress of the students, what plan of action would you develop keeping in mind the Effective Schools Research?

Effective Schools Reference List

Anderson, L, Everstson, C. and Brophy, J. (1979). An experimental study of effective teaching in first grade reading groups. *The Elementary School Journal*, 79, 193 - 222.

Berliner,D. (1984). The half-full glass: a review of research on teaching. *Using what we know about teaching*. Alexandria, Va.: Association for Supervision and Curriculum Development.

Best, J. (1977). *Research in education*. Englewood Cliffs : Prentice Hall.

Billups, L. and Rauth, M. (1984). The new research: how effective teachers teach. *American Educator*, Summer, 39.

Brookover, W.B. and et al. (1979). *School systems and student achievement: schools make a difference*. New York: Prager.

Brookover, W.B. and Lezotte, L.W. (1979). Changes in school characteristics coincident with changes in student achievement. East Lansing: Michigan State (Unpublished paper) ED 181 005.

Brophy, J. (1979). Classroom organization and management. *Elementary School Journal*, March.

Brophy, J. (1979). Teacher behavior and its effects. *Journal of Educational Psychology*, 71, 733-750.

Cahn, S. (1982). The art of teaching. *American Educator*, Fall.

ED-LINE News Briefs. (1987). May.

Edmonds, R. (1979). Effective schools for urban poor. *Educational Leadership*, 37, 15 - 24.

Farrar, E. et al. (1984). Effective schools programming high schools: social promotion or movement by merit. *Phi Delta Kappa*, June.

Fisher et al. (1980). Teaching behaviors, academic learning time and student achievement: An overview. *Time to Learn*. Washington, D.C.: NIE.

Good, T. (1975).*Teachers make a difference*. New York: Holt, Rinehart and Winston.

Good, T. and Brophy, J. (1978). *Looking in classrooms*. New York: Harper and Row.

Idol-Maestas, L. (1986). Teaching middle school students to use a test-taking strategy. *Journal of Educational Research*, 79,350-357.

Levine, D.U. and Lezotte, L.W. (1990). *Unusually Effective Schools*. Washington, D.C: National Center for Effective Schools Research and Development.

Meir, D. (1984). Getting tough in schools. *Dissent*, Winter, 61-70.

Prince, S.B. and Taylor, R.G. (1995). Should the correlates of effective schools be used as a prescription for improving achievement? *Educational Research Quarterly*, 18 (4), 19-25.

Purkey, S. and Smith, M. (1982). Too soon to cheer? synthesis of research on effective schools. *Educational Leadership*, 64-69.

Resnick, D. and Resnick, L. (1985). Standards curriculum and performance: historical comparative perspectives. *Educational Researcher*, 14, 5-20.

Rosenshine, B. (1979). Content time and direct instruction. *Research on teaching: Concepts, findings and implications*. Berkley, Calif.: McCutchan.

Rosenshine, B. (1983). Teaching functions in instructional programs. *Elementary School Journal*, March.

Rutherford, W. (1985). School principals as effective leaders. *Phi Delta Kappa*, 31-34.

Rutter, M. et al. (1979). *Fifteen thousand hours: Secondary schools and their effects on children.* Cambridge: Harvard University Press.

Stedman, L. (1987). It's time we changed the effective schools formula. *Phi Delta Kappa,* November, 215-224.

Wallberg, H. (1988). Synthesis of research on time and learning. *Educational Leadership,* 45, 76-85.

RESTRUCTURING/IMPROVING
THE SCHOOLS EXERCISE

Goal: To suggest and recommend ways American schools
                 may be restructured and improved.

Objectives: The student will develop a plan consisting of
                 suggestions and recommendations for restructuring
                 and improving the schools in his/her community,
                 region, or state.

Premises:

1) The nation-wide political thrust in education in preparation for the 21st century calls for a restructuring of the American schools.
2) This thrust for restructuring is based upon a perceived need to improve the quality of American education so that the students of the American schools will be competitive with the students of schools throughout the world.
3) The improvement in the quality of education in America is based upon a major concern that the American economy must remain competitive with the thriving and developing economies of other nations throughout the world.

Input:

Restructuring the American schools seems to be the most recent political theme for the 1990's. Even many educational groups and leaders are calling for a restructuring of the American schools. But what does restructuring mean?

For some people restructuring means that parents should be given a choice as to which school they may send their children. For others restructuring may also include the formation of local school governing councils such as now used in the Chicago Public Schools. It also means for many teacher union leaders, the active participation of teachers in the decision making process both at the district level as well as at the school campus level.

The report from the Carnegie Forum on Education and the Economy *A Nation Prepared: Teachers for the 21st Century* calls for a change in the goals of American education from those serving an economy based on mass production to those goals addressing the need to prepare students for the knowledge industries. In this context, the report says that the schools must stop teaching repetitive skills needed in mass production and start teaching higher level thinking skills to students. This position is reiterated in the U.S. Labor Department's, *What Work Requires of Schools - A Scans Report for America 2000* (1992).

The GOALS 2000: Educate America Act established the following eight National Education Goals for the year 2000:

1) All children in America will start school ready to learn.
2) The high school graduation rate will increase to at least 90 percent.
3) All students will leave grades 4, 8, and 12 having demonstrated competency over challenging subject matter including English, mathematics, science, foreign languages, civics and government, economics, arts, history, and geography, and every school in America will ensure that all students learn to use their minds well, so they may be prepared for responsible citizenship, further learning, and productive employment in our Nation's modern economy.
4) The Nation's teaching force will have access to programs for the continued improvement of their professional skills and the opportunity to acquire the knowledge and skills needed to instruct and prepare all American students for the next century.
5) U.S. students will be first in the world in mathematics and science achievement.
6) Every adult American will be literate and will possess the knowledge and skills necessary to compete in a global economy and exercise the rights and responsibilities of citizenship.
7) Every school in the United States will be free of drugs, violence, and the unauthorized presence of firearms and alcohol and will offer a disciplined environment conducive to learning.
8) Every school will promote partnerships that will increase parental involvement and participation in promoting the social, emotional, and academic growth of children.

So from whatever source, educational or political, the call is for the schools to change. The call is for schools to improve so that our students will be competitive with the students from throughout the world as we enter the 21st century. That the U.S. economy will be on the par with or superior to that of Japan, Germany, and other economically thriving countries is a major concern to those calling for a restructuring of American schools.

But how this restructuring is to be done is controversial, maybe costly, and definitely ill-defined.

Activity:

Develop a plan consisting of specific suggestions and recommendations for restructuring and improving the schools in your community, region, and/or state. Consider choice options, governance options, new teaching and learning strategies, new curriculum programs, different school program funding options, and any other ideas which would lead to educational improvement.

Reference

Carnegie Forum on Education and the Economy. (1986). *A nation prepared: Teachers for the 21st century.* New York: Carnegie Corporation.

United States Department of Labor. (1992). *What work requires of schools.* (029-000-00433-1) Pittsburgh, PA: US Government Bookstore.

PREPARING FOR SUCCESS EXERCISES

This set of exercises focuses on several personal and professional skills the student should develop in his/her pursuit of an administrative position. The first two exercises in this set pertain to skills in writing memoranda and in developing proposals. Principals prepare numerous memos to staff and frequently must prepare proposals to the superintendent of schools and/or other central administrators for new programs. These two exercises will help the student develop these vital skills before going into the principal's position.

The final exercises in this section focus on being prepared to get a job as an assistant principal or principal. Thus, having one's credentials prepared, possessing a well-organized portfolio, knowing one's career objectives, being well-read and educationally *"literate"* are just some basics which must be mastered in preparing oneself for an administrative position in today's competitive marketplace.

DOCUMENTATION MEMORANDA EXERCISE

Goal: To develop a written memorandum for documentation purposes on personnel matters.

Objective: The student will write a summary memorandum for documentation purposes.

Premises:

1) Memoranda provide both parties with a common understanding of the incident or issue.
2) A well written memorandum provides documentation that transcends time and will withstand judicial review.

Input:

There are different types of memoranda:

1) Memorandum to file - A record of a minor problem which involves a teacher or other employee.
2) Specific incident memorandum - A principal observes an incident or has a complaint from a third party and thus sends a teacher a memorandum regarding the incident/complaint.
3) Visitation memorandum - A summary of a classroom visit by the principal or supervisor.
4) Summary memorandum - An outline of the results of several incidents and/or classroom observations.

It is good practice to precede a memorandum with a personnel conference to establish the validity of the content of the documentation.

A well written memorandum will adhere to the following format:

1) Specifies to whom memo is being sent.
2) States who is sending the memo.
3) States the subject matter of the memo.
4) States date of the memo.

Example:
```
TO:       Joe Know-It-All
FROM:     Paul Principal
RE:       Classroom Visitation
DATE:     January 14, 199_
```

The memo content should be:
1) Factual
2) Job specific
3) Dated as to when incident/observation occurred
4) Prepared in the first person (You and I)
5) Non inflammatory and/or non judgmental
6) Signed by preparer of memo

In certain situations, it may be necessary to ask the teacher to sign the memo, acknowledging receiving and reading the memo. The signature of the teacher does not necessarily mean that the teacher agrees with the content of the memo.

Activity:

Write a summary memorandum based on the following memoranda on file:

Teacher: Mr. Know-It-All
School: Anywhere High School
Grade: 9th
Subject: History

9/20/9_   Did not sign in upon arriving at school 8:20 - 15 minutes late (Principal)

9/25/9_   Did not show up for faculty meeting (Principal)

9/30/9_   Did not turn in lesson plans till Tuesday p.m. (Secretary)

10/5/9_   Did not show up for lunchroom duty as assigned (Assistant Principal)

PROPOSAL WRITING EXERCISE

Goal: To develop a written proposal.

Objectives:

1) The student will select a topic (curricular, instructional, or programmatic) from the five year goals of the strategic plan.
2) The student will do a task analysis and address the development, implementation and evaluation of the topic.
3) The student will write a proposal not to exceed two pages.

Premises:

1) A proposal is a systematic presentation of an idea under consideration.
2) A proposal should be:
   a) Comprehensive in scope: all possible questions and concerns addressed
   b) Logical in format
   c) Parallel in written construction: narrative or outline form

Input:

A proposal is an attempt to present in a systematic way a concept for implementation. It may address a concept in the area of instruction, curriculum or program. Each proposal is unique and is developed for the specific objective to be accomplished.

Some possible areas to include in a proposal are as follows:

1) Goal
2) Objectives
3) Rationale
4) Background
5) Logistics
6) Resources (monetary, time and human)
7) Benefits to the organization

8) Benefits to the individual
9) Evaluation

Activity:

Write a two page proposal to implement a concept in the area of instruction, curriculum or program. Examples of topics could be:

1) Improve standardized test scores
2) Implement an at-risk program
3) Institute a critical thinking skills curriculum

PROFESSIONAL CREDENTIALS EXERCISE

Goal: To prepare professional credentials for use in applying for an administrative position.

Objectives:

1) The student will prepare a cover letter.
2) The student will prepare an educational resume.

Premises:

1) The development of a set of professional credentials is a prerequisite for securing an administrative position.
2) The credential file allows the prospective employer to screen applicants to determine if the applicants possess the desired attributes for the position.
3) The credential file provides the prospective applicant an opportunity to project a positive image.
4) A credential file may consist of the following documents:
   a) Cover Letter
   b) Resume
   c) Letters of Reference

Input:

A cover letter usually accompanies professional credentials and is designed to express the applicant's interest in the position. In addition, it provides the applicant an opportunity to demonstrate his/her writing proficiency. A typical cover letter may consist of the following components:

1) Introduction - Paragraph expressing interest in the position.
2) Body - A series of paragraphs stating qualifications for the position. The qualifications stated in the letter should be supplemental to the qualifications included in the resume. The content of the letter should not be repetitive of the qualifications in the resume, but possibly it could further explain or expand the applicant's qualifications listed in the

86

resume.

3) Conclusion - A paragraph indicating the desire to meet with the employer to discuss the position. The letter should be approximately one page in length and adhere to acceptable business format. The key to a cover letter is that it be positive and professional.

The second component of the professional credentials is the educational resume. It is designed to project in writing a comprehensive profile of an individual's qualifications. A resume typically consists of the following areas:

1) Personal Data - Demographic data such as address, home phone number, business phone number.
2) Education - Universities attended, degrees held, dates of degrees.
3) Educational Experiences - Teaching and administrative experiences. List title of position, name and address of employer, and dates of experiences.
4) References - Professional references (present and former supervisors, university professors, colleagues). Include place of employment, address and business phone number of references.

In addition to the aforementioned areas an applicant may choose to include other items which project positively on his/her candidacy such as:

1) Professional Achievements - Publications and presentations made at conventions and workshops
2) Honors/Awards - Special recognition received (educational, civic, other)
3) Civic/Religious Involvement - Membership and leadership roles assumed in civic or religious organizations
4) Professional Associations - Membership and leadership roles in professional associations
5) Other Areas - Qualities or experiences that are unique such as bilingual qualifications, military experience, private sector experience, etc.

87

The resume should be organized in a logical format typically with strengths listed first to project a positive image. Other considerations in the preparation of a resume include leaving sufficient white space so the document does not appear cluttered, and using a good quality bond paper. With the advent of computers it is very easy to produce a professionally looking resume that can be updated easily with new information as the need arises.

Many universities have placement offices that will assist students in establishing and maintaining professional credential files for use in securing a position.

Activities:

1) The student will prepare a cover letter for an administrative position.
2) The student will prepare a resume to accompany the cover letter.

Optional Activity:

The student will contact the university placement office to establish a credential file.

COVER LETTER WORKSHEET

Paragraph One - Express interest in the position

Paragraph Two - Discuss skills related to the position

Paragraph Three - Discuss personal attributes

Paragraph Four - Close the letter

Cover Letter Checklist
1) inside address
2) left justified format
3) block style
4) one page in length
5) typed or letter quality printer
6) bond paper - 24 lbs.
7) color paper (optional) - buff, light green, light blue, or light gray
8) correct spelling
9) correct punctuation and grammar

LOOKS PROFESSIONAL   SOUNDS PROFESSIONAL

RESUME WORKSHEET

Step One - Gather the Information

Personal Data - name, address, phone number(s)

Job Objective - optional

Educational Background - colleges, addresses, degrees, specializations

Certifications - teacher, administrator

Work Experience - teaching, administrative

Specialized Training/Workshops (optional)

Professional Organizations (optional)

Activities and Awards - educational, civic, religious (optional)

Professional References - name, position, address, telephone number

Step Two - Arrange the Information

Step Three - Finished Product Checklist
1) white space - not cluttered
2) block style
3) bond paper - 24 lbs.
4) color paper - buff, light green, light blue, or light gray (optional)
5) two pages in length
6) correct spelling
7) correct punctuation
8) correct grammatically

FORMAL   **FACTUAL**   **CONCISE**

EDUCATIONAL ADMINISTRATION
PORTFOLIO EXERCISE

Goal:
To prepare an educational administration portfolio to use as an employment tool for obtaining an administrative position.

Objectives:
The student will develop and/or organize selected items into an educational administration portfolio.

Premises:

1) A portfolio can be used for one of two purposes:
   a) as an evaluation and development tool.
   b) as an employment tool.
2) The portfolio allows an administrative candidate the opportunity to share information with prospective employers that would not otherwise be available to them.
3) The portfolio provides the student with a mechanism for projecting a positive perception of his/her qualifications during an interview.

Input:

Educators typically think of a portfolio as a tool for student and/or faculty evaluation and development. Institutions (K-12 and higher education) are utilizing portfolios as an alternative or as a complement to the existing assessment process.

However in other professional fields the portfolio is used as an employment tool. The portfolio would serve as a representative body of work to support the candidate's qualifications for a position. The employment portfolio should include selected pieces of work that correlate with potential success in the position for which the candidate is applying.

The educational administration portfolio could include the following:

1) Introductory Section
   a) Cover Letter

      b) Resume
2)   Main Body - Selected items from *The Principal's Companion*
      such as:
      a) Strategic Planning Model
      b) Discipline Management Plan
      c) Public Relations Plan
      d) School Assessment Surveys
      e) Documentation Memorandum
      f) Proposal Writing Exercise
3)   Supplemental Materials - Optional
      a) Photographs
      b) Newspaper Clippings

The portfolio should be professional. Suggestions include:

1)   Placing materials in a three ring binder
2)   Using bond paper for items
3)   Incorporating graphics and visuals
4)   Using a laser quality printer
5)   Tabbing the major sections
6)   Developing a table of contents

Activities:

Develop an educational administration portfolio to be used as an
employment tool with the following sections:

1)   Introduction
      a) Table of Contents
      b) Cover Letter
      c) Resume
2)   Main Body - Selected work from the *The Principal's
      Companion* and other sources (classwork) that correlates with
      your administrative aspirations
3)   Supplemental Materials - Include information as needed

PERSONAL AND PROFESSIONAL
CAREER PLANNING EXERCISE

Goal: To identify short, medium and long range personal and professional goals.

Objective: The student will develop a list of short, medium, and long range personal and professional goals.

Premises:

1) Goal setting is an organizational and personal tool designed to improve productivity and quality of life.
2) Professional and personal goal setting is a vital function if an individual is to experience growth.
3. Goal setting provides a focus for the individual to channel energy and a way to evaluate success.

Input:

Success has been defined as the satisfactory attainment of our goals in life. In essence, without goals one cannot have a focus to evaluate success. Goals can fall into two major categories:

1) Personal goals are those that relate to the individual, his/her family or to personal interests.
2) Professional goals are those that relate to one's career.

Goals may be projected in a time framework as follows:

1) Short range - less than six months
2) Medium range - six months to three years
3) Long range - three years to ten years

In the establishment of professional goals it is important to ask yourself the following questions:

1) What would I like to be doing next year? three years? five years?
2) What do I need to do to accomplish these goals (i.e. in terms of additional education, experiences, certification, etc.)?

In essence, goals form the outline and framework for effective personal and career planning.

Activity:

Complete the goal worksheet.

GOAL EXERCISE WORKSHEET

1) Make a list of your goals (things you want to accomplish).

2) Arrange the goals into two lists, one for personal goals and the other for professional goals.

3) Identify each goal as:
    a) short range - less than six months
    b) medium range - six months to three years
    c) long range - three years to ten years

4) Prioritize the goals in each category in numerical order from those of greatest to least importance.

5) Write a goal statement for each goal using the following sentence stem:
    a) Within the next three months I will...
    b) Within the next six months to three years 1 will..
    c) Within the next three years to ten years I will...

6) Select your number one goal from each category and identify a plan of action for accomplishing the goal, i.e. time line for activities, resources such as time and money needed, etc.

95

PROFESSIONAL GROWTH PLAN EXERCISE

Goal: To develop a personal professional growth plan.

Objective: The student will develop a personal growth plan consisting of the identification of a mentor and a list of professional readings.

Premises:

1) The knowledge base that is comprised in the field of educational administration continues to evolve at a rapid rate.
2) The completion of an administrative preparatory program is only the initial step in the development of future administrators.
3) Professional development is related to the following goals:
   a) improving performance in current position
   b) developing skills for anticipated vacancies
   c) promoting self-development/self-actualization
4) Future administrators must take the initiative to establish a plan for their continual professional development.

Input:

One strategy for promoting professional growth is to identify a mentor to serve as a role model and teacher for the future administrator. A mentor is someone who possesses the conceptual, technical and human relations skills necessary for success in the field. Under the tutelage and guidance of the mentor the student can observe and acquire experiences that assist in professional development. In addition the mentor quite frequently will serve as an advocate for the individual as he/she seeks a position.

The second strategy is to engage in professional reading. The reading should occur in three basic areas. The first area in which to read is professional journals and newspapers as well as books in the field of education and educational administration. Professional journals could include the *Educational Leadership*, *Kappan*, and other notable

96

publications. A popular professional newspaper is the *Education Week*. The second category is current writing in the field of management, organizational theory, and leadership. These books are written typically for the private sector. Many of them are currently popular and may be identified from best seller's lists found in major newspapers such as *The New York Times*. The final area is to read daily newspapers and weekly news magazines to stay abreast of educational developments nationally, state-wide, and locally.

In the final analysis professional growth is ultimately the responsibility of the future administrator.

Activity: On the attached sheet prepare a professional growth
                 plan.

PROFESSIONAL GROWTH PLAN

I. Mentor:

    1) Who will serve as your mentor?

    2) What is the rationale for selecting that person?

    3) What specific skills (conceptual, technical, human relations) do you hope to develop through your association with this individual?

    4) How will you use this person?

II. Professional Readings

    1) Journals/Newspapers/Books   Time line
       a)
       b)
       c)
       d)

    2. Management Publications   Time line
       a)
       b)
       c)
       d)

    3. Newspapers and Magazines   Time line
       a)
       b)

98

READING LIST FOR THE 21st CENTURY

Goal: To read, analyze and apply current research and thought in the area of leadership theory to educational settings.

Objective: The student will read a book from the attached list.

Premises:

1) A majority of research in management and leadership is conducted in the private sector.
2) Educational administrators should read literature from the private sector and analyze the theories, concepts, and strategies to see if they are applicable to educational institutions.

Activity:

1) Read a book from the attached list.
2) Identify the central themes of the book.
3) Discuss the application of the central themes to the principalship.

Reading List For The 21st Century

Barker, J.A. (1992). *Future edge.* New York: William and Morrow Company.

Bennis, W. and Nanus, B. (1985). *Leaders.* New York: Harper and Row.

Bennis, W. (1989). *Why leaders can't lead.* San Francisco: Jossey-Bass Publishers.

Bennis, W. and Miscne, M. (1995). *The 21st century organization.* San Diego: Pfeiffer & Company.

Bennis, W. (1989). *On becoming a leader.* Reading, Massachusetts: Addison Wesley Publishing Company.

Blanchard, K. and Johnson, S. (1981). *The one minute manager.* New York: Berkley Books.

Blanchard, K. and Peale, N. (1988). *The power of ethical management.* New York: Fawcett Crest.

Blanchard, K., Zigarmi, P. and Zigmari,D. (1985). *Leadership and the one minute manager.* New York: William Morrow and Company.

Burns, J. (1979). *Leadership.* New York: Harper and Row.

Cetron, M. and Gayle, M. (1991). *Educational renaissance.* New York: St. Martin's Press

Covey, S.(1989). *The 7 habits of highly effective people.* New York: Simon & Schuster.

Covey, S. (1994). *First things first.* New York: Simon & Schuster.

Drucker, P. (1985). *The effective executive.* New York: Harper and Row Publishers.

Garfield, Charles. (1987). *Peak performers.* New York: Avon Books.

Hersey, P. and Blanchard, K. (1988). *Management of organizational behavior*. Englewood Cliffs: Prentice Hall.

Hirsch, E.D. (1987). *Cultural literacy : what every American should know*. Boston: Houghton Mifflin Company.

Katzenbach, J. and Smith, D. (1993). *The wisdom of teams*. New York: Harper Collins.

Lewis, A. (1989). *Restructuring America's schools*. Arlington: American Association of School Administrators.

Mayer, J. (1990). *If you haven't got the time to do it right, when will you find the time to do it over ?* New York: Simon & Schuster.

Manning, G.; Curtis, K. and McMillen, S. (1996). *Building community: the human side of work*. Cincinnati, Ohio: Thomas Executive Press.

March, J. (1994). *A primer on decision making*. New York: The Free Press.

McFarland, L. et.al. (1994). *21st century leadership*. New York: The Leadership Press.

Naisbitt, J. and Aburdene, P. (1990). *Megatrends 2000*. New York: William Morrow Company.

Nanus, B. (1989). *The leader's edge*. Chicago: Contemporary Books Inc.

Nanus, B. (1992). *Visionary leadership*. San Francisco: Jossey-Bass publishers.

O'Toole, J. (1995). *Leading change*. San Francisco: Jossey-Bass Press.

Peters, T.J. (1987). *Thriving on chaos*. New York: Alfred A. Knopf.

Peters, T.J. and Waterman, R. Jr. (1982). *In search of excellence*. New York: Harper and Row.

Smith, W. and Andrews, R. (1989). *Instructional leadership: how principals make a difference*. Alexandria: Association for supervision and Curriculum Development.

Ziglar, Z. (1986). *Top performance*. New Jersey: Fleming H. Revell Company.

EDUCATIONAL ADMINISTRATION
LITERACY EXERCISE

Goal: To become familiar with terms, concepts, and theories that form the foundation of educational administration.

Objectives: The student will be able to explain the terms, concepts and theories.

Premises:

1) In a literate society there are terms and concepts that are universally understood. These terms facilitate the communication of ideas.
2) There are certain terms, concepts and theories that are generally accepted as comprising the foundation of educational administration.
3) It is incumbent upon students of educational administration to be knowledgeable about these terms, concepts and theories that comprise basic educational administration literacy.

Input:

E.D. Hirsch in his book *Cultural Literacy* (1987) presented the argument that there is a set of terms and concepts that comprise a storehouse of knowledge that a literate person possesses. Furthermore, the fact that these terms are universally understood by literate individuals facilitates communication between these individuals. For instance, when one speaks of "The Father of Our Country," it is universally accepted that one is referring to George Washington.

Each profession has its own unique set of terms, concepts and theories that are accepted as comprising basic foundational knowledge in that area. Thus, a practicing educational administrator would need to be familiar with the terms, concepts and theories that comprise the basis for educational administration literacy. For instance, an administrator who was described as a "Theory Y" administrator would create a common understanding in both the sender and the receiver as to what

103

type of administrative style is preferred by the individual. In essence the body of knowledge facilitates the communication of ideas.

Activity:

Define the terms, concepts and theories listed below.

EDUCATIONAL ADMINISTRATION
LITERACY TERMS

TERMS

accountability

at-risk

authoritarian leadership

bureaucracy

campus-based management

charter schools

climate

cooperation

correlates of effective schools

decision making

delegation

democratic leadership

due process

effectiveness

efficiency

empowerment

equal protection clause

equity in school finance

First Amendment

formal organization

formative evaluation

Fourteenth Amendment

freedom of choice

Hawthorne Effect

home schooling

human relations period

hypothesis

inclusion (special education)

in loco parentis

informal organization

instructional leadership

interdisciplinary teaching

job latitude

job thickness

key communicators

liberty interests

line and staff

locus of control

Management by Objectives (MBO's)

models

motivation (content and process)

normative evaluation

outcome based education

paradigms

participative leadership

policy and regulation

property rights

responsibility

restructuring schools

scientific approach

scientific management

site-based management

situational leadership

social systems

span of control

standardized achievement test

subordinate

summative evaluation

superordinate

supervision (clinical and developmental)

the three part test regarding state-church issues

theory

transformational leadership

vision

voucher system

year-round school

MODELS AND THEORIES

Equity Theory

Expectancy Theory

Getzels-Guba Model

Goal Path

Herzberg Motivation and Hygiene Theory

Johari Window

Katz Model

Managerial Grid

Maslow's Hierarchy

Theory X and Theory Y

Theory Z

Total Quality Management

IN-BASKET SIMULATIONS

The next section of this book contains numerous in-basket simulations which attempt to exemplify the types of problems the principal encounters in his/her management of the school. All of these examples have actually occurred in the schools of the authors or in schools from which our graduate students are teachers or administrators. The names have been changed, some editing on memos and phone messages has occurred, but the basic situations are as close to what actually happened as we can describe them.

We believe the situations are typical, if situations a principal encounters each day can be described as typical. Some may require little response on the part of the students, yet others may require a lengthy and complex response. The type of response may depend upon the situation and how the simulations are being used in a class. But we can assure you, there are no right or wrong answers; only you and your professor can determine what is the best response given the situation.

IN-BASKET SIMULATIONS

Goal: To demonstrate skills in solving and handling problems and items faced by principals in the daily management of the schools.

Objectives:

1) The student will demonstrate administrative and leadership skills in solving/handling various problems faced daily by principals.
2) The student will demonstrate skills in communicating with others as situations are handled in the school setting.

Premises:

1) Administrators must make decisions, and how these decisions are made is as important in most cases as what the decisions are.
2) Decision making is a risky process since the selected decision may turn-out wrong. The effective administrator will be prepared to handle the situation if the decision is wrong.
3) Involving those who are affected by the problem, who are impacted by the solution to the problem, who are concerned about the problem, and who are responsible for implementing the solution is an absolute necessity. Commitment to successfully solving the problem is based upon involving people who are impacted by the problem.

Input:

There are several decision making/problem solving models found in the leadership literature. One model found to be effective involves seven steps:

1) **Identify the problem** - the most crucial step because some people tend to guise the real problem behind ambiguous statements and questions. Probing the person with the

110

problem helps draw out a better definition of the problem.

2) **Gather the facts** - helps to better define the problem, involves people who care about the problem and who are a part of the problem and the solution. Judgment has to be made as to how much time is available to gather facts.

3) **Generate alternative solutions** - solutions from doing nothing to do everything possible should be considered. Brainstorming is used here. No idea is bad. One person's idea may help someone else think of another idea, possibly a better idea.

4) **Consider implications and consequences of the alternative solutions** - the amount of time needed, available money, number of available people and the kinds of skills available, politics of the situation, community values and traditions are just a few of the factors to be considered at this stage. Question to ask is "What happens if we do...?"

5) **Select a solution** - made by appropriate decision makers based on a consensus of the people involved in steps 1-4. May not be the "best" solution as perceived by some people but it is the best solution perceived by all people involved in the situation. Solutions may not "maximize" the situation, may only "satisfy" the situation.

6) **Implement the solution** - involves people who are impacted by and care about the problem, who have been involved in seeking a solution, and who are responsible for solving the problem. These people should have reached a level of high commitment in order to successfully carry-out a solution to solve the problem.

7) **Evaluate the solution** - should be a planned process involving the people who implemented the solution as well as others impacted by the problem and solution. Question of "Did the selected solution work as planned?" should be answered. If the selected solution did not work, or at least work to the desired level, then the decision making/problem solving process starts over. Rarely is the problem the same as it was in the beginning, particularly after a selected solution has failed. It is a new problem!

111

Several major factors to consider in evaluating one's performance in dealing with in-basket simulations come from research done by assessment centers (See note below). Assessment center technology attempts to provide perspective administrators with simulations of situations that typically occur in an organization. The performance of the individual is then evaluated based on criteria that have been identified as having a high correlation with successful operation of an organization. These skills include:

1) Decisiveness - ability to act when a decision is required
2) Judgment - ability to make sound, rational decisions
3) Time Management - ability to organize and handle tasks in an efficient and systematic way
4) Problem Solving - ability to analyze the various components of a situation
5) Leadership - ability to direct others to accomplish the task
6) Interpersonal - ability to display sensitivity for others
7) Stress Tolerance - the ability to handle stress in a productive way
8) Oral communication - ability to express ideas effectively in oral communication
9) Written Communication - ability to express ideas effectively in written communication

Note: The aforementioned areas are extracted from a variety of assessment center models including: **American Management Association, National Association of Secondary Schools Principals, and Assessment Designs, Incorporated.**

IN-BASKET SIMULATION #1

Good Morning M. Principal

You arrive early to school one morning. You visit with several teachers, talk to some students, and walk through the entire school. In the early days of the school year, all seems to be going smoothly.

You return to your office, and you find the following note on your desk:

To	_M. Principal_
Date _9-13-9-_	Time _8:30 a.m._

WHILE YOU WERE OUT

M ___Mary Davis___

of ___parent___

Phone (____) __555-1717__
Area Code   Number   Extension

TELEPHONE	X	PLEASE CALL	X
CALLED TO SEE YOU		WILL CALL AGAIN	
WANTS TO SEE YOU		URGENT	
RETURNED YOUR CALL			

Message _Says her son was hit and kicked by another_ _student on the way to school this morning. The son,_ _Jeff, returned home. She has taken him to the_ _hospital._

___Sharon___
Operator

IN-BASKET SIMULATION #2

Surprise Package

A parent comes to school and requests that you return the box of tissues his child brought as part of his school supplies. The counselor goes to fetch the box and notices that it appears to be open. When she looks inside, she is surprised to find what appears to be a small bag of marijuana.

What is your next move?

IN-BASKET SIMULATION #3

Complaint From Teachers

TO: M. Principal
FROM: Social Studies Teachers
SUBJECT: Delores Bowman
           Clerical Aide
DATE: October 10, 199_

We want to call your attention to the improper and sometimes unethical behavior of Mrs. Delores Bowman, our clerical aide.

She is curt and disrespectful at times. She sasses us on occasion and she is not always helpful to us. She frequently goes to teachers who have her son in class and questions them about why they are doing certain things and why her son is not doing better in their classes.

Mrs. Bowman is not always on time with her work and we must correct most of the work she does for us.

We would like for you to do something about Mrs. Bowman.

IN-BASKET SIMULATION #4

Breaking the Sound Barrier

John Clark is a first year, fourth grade teacher, teaching in a basement classroom in the elementary school. The floor is hardwood, the ceiling is high and non-acoustical, and the walls are plaster. All sounds in the room vibrate greatly.

As you have walked the hallways, you have noticed that Mr. Clark's voice is very loud, and can be heard several rooms away, even when his classroom door is closed. At times, Mr. Clark shouts at the students to get quiet, to take their seats, and to get busy with their homework.

When you visit his classroom, you notice that the students are restless, things are frequently dropped on the hardwood floor, making loud cracking sounds, and the general tone of the classroom is noisy and uncomfortable.

You are bothered by the whole scene.

The Concerned Mother

As you were leaving school late yesterday afternoon, Mrs. Jeanne Cross, the English teacher, met you in the hallway, and told you of a difficult conference she just had with Mrs. Dull, mother of Joey.

Mrs. Cross said that Mrs. Dull does not understand how the homework and classwork are graded, and that she (Mrs. Dull) feels that Joey's grades ought to be higher. Mrs. Cross also said that Joey works hard, tries to do the assignments, but that his work is usually incomplete and unsatisfactory.

This morning you return to the office and find this telephone message:

To	*M. Principal*
Date	*10-23-9-* Time *9:15 a.m.*

WHILE YOU WERE OUT

M   *Mrs. Dull*

of   *Joey's mother*

Phone (   )   *555-2930*
     Area Code   Number   Extension

TELEPHONE	X	PLEASE CALL	X
CALLED TO SEE YOU		WILL CALL AGAIN	
WANTS TO SEE YOU		URGENT	
	RETURNED YOUR CALL		

Message   *Concerned about Joey's low grade in English. Says he is already two grades behind in school. What can she do?*

                   Sharon
                   Operator

IN-BASKET SIMULATION #6

The Unhappy Foreign Student

Yhi-Min Ho is a student from Taiwan attending your high school under the American Field Service program. He arrived in August after attending an orientation in New York, and was placed with a family with two boys, Geoffrey and Gregory Karna, who also attend your high school.

Yhi-Min is a very quiet boy, very studious, and after two months of living in your community, he is quite homesick. He rarely attends after school and community activities, but he does seem to enjoy the AFS activities where he has had the opportunity to see several other students from his homeland.

On the other hand, Geoffrey and Gregory Karna are almost opposites of Yhi-Min. Both are very popular in school, active in various sports and club activities, above average students, and are always on the go. Geoffrey, a senior, is president of the student council and captain of the basketball team. Gregory, a sophomore, also plays basketball, is a member of the student council, and is one of the reporters on the school newspaper.

Mrs. Anna Welder, one of the foreign language teachers in your school, is the sponsor of the AFS program. On Monday morning before school begins, she visits you in your office to tell you what happened with Yhi-Min over the weekend.

It seems that on one of the AFS weekend trips, Yhi-Min told several other AFS students that he hated his American family, that he hated the school, and that he was going to leave as soon as he could return to Taiwan.

One of the AFS sponsors on the trip learned of Yhi-Min's comments and called Mrs. Welder on Sunday evening. Mrs. Welder says she has not talked to Yhi-Min or the Karna family. She first wants to discuss with you what should be done.

118

IN-BASKET SIMULATION #7

Letter From Mother

October 28, 199_

Dear M. Principal:

I want to make you aware of a very serious problem that we as parents of Johnny are encountering with Mrs. Roberts, Johnny's teacher.

For the third time this month, Mrs. Roberts has kept Johnny after school as punishment for what she called "classroom misbehavior." One time he was chewing gum, another time he was late for class, and the third time he was talking to some other students in the class.

Of course we want Johnny to behave in school and we understand the importance of discipline, but it is unreasonable to expect parents to have to provide special transportation so that the teacher can keep our son after school. If the teacher would exercise better control in the classroom, it would not be necessary for her to keep children after school.

I am sure you understand our problem, and will look into the matter and take action to correct this unnecessary inconvenience on our part.

Thank you very much.

Sincerely yours,

Betty Byers

IN BASKET SIMULATION #8

Separation of Church and State Or Freedom of Distribution

Members of the Gideons have visited your office on several occasions requesting permission to distribute the King James Version of the Bible to your students. Each time you have told them that school board policy prohibits the distribution of religious materials to students by non-school groups. On the last visit, one of the members of the group said that he personally had talked to several school board trustees and all favored the distribution. The member, Henry Goodwork, further declared that the Gideons would distribute the Bibles one way or another. Soon after your morning cup of coffee, your secretary hands you the following telephone message:

To _____ *M. Principal* _____

Date_____ *11-1-9-* _____ Time _____ *9:15 a.m.* _____

WHILE YOU WERE OUT

M _____ *Pastor Goodwork* _____

of _____

Phone (____) _____ *555-6329* _____

Area Code   Number   Extension

TELEPHONE	X	PLEASE CALL	X
CALLED TO SEE YOU		WILL CALL AGAIN	
WANTS TO SEE YOU		URGENT	
	RETURNED YOUR CALL		

Message _*Members of congregation will be passing out*_
*copies of the Bible to High School students tomorrow*
*in parking lot.*

_____

_____

_____ *Sharon* _____
Operator

IN-BASKET SIMULATION #9

The Lunch Bunch

Note found on desk upon your return from Chamber of Commerce luncheon:

M. Principal:

Two boys, Mick Moseley and Robbie Cox, were fighting in the cafeteria at noon. No reason given by boys. Robbie received a bloody nose; nurse took care of him. Mick was unhurt.

I told the boys you would paddle them when you got back.

Hank Rambo
11-12-9_

(Mr. Rambo is the boys physical education teacher)

IN-BASKET SIMULATION #10

Phone Call From Board Member

You received a call from a school board member last night (November 20, 199_) telling you that Mr. Armstrong, one of your teachers, has been slapping kids in his class. The board member's son was one of the kids.

He wants immediate action, and he asked you to call him as to your action ASAP.

IN-BASKET SIMULATION #11

The Disappearing Food

On one of your daily walks through the school, Mrs. Jewell, the cafeteria manager, asks you to come into her office for a private discussion. She then tells you that left-over food placed in the cooler located in the back of the kitchen area has been disappearing. She says the cooler is always locked after clean-up each day, and only she, Mr. Mac., the head custodian, and the superintendent have keys to the cooler.

Mrs. Jewell says the amount of food is not very great, but on occasion containers of chili, containers of potatoes, and two or three large meat packages have disappeared.

Two ladies assist Mrs. Jewell in the cafeteria, and occasionally, parent volunteers will assist when special meals are prepared. Mrs. Jewell says the other workers always leave before or with her at the end of each work day, and thus are not likely suspects to be taking food with them.

She adds she has not discussed the matter with anyone else, but she does not know what to do about the problem. She says it is costing the cafeteria program money, and she adds that she needs your help to stop the disappearances.

Teacher Accolade

As principal, you have been active in the local chamber of commerce. Through your efforts, programs have been initiated to give recognition to teachers and students for their accomplishments. Due to family illness, you were unable to attend the annual chamber banquet last night. However the following message was on your desk after lunch regarding one of your teachers:

To _____ *M. Principal* _____

Date _____ *12-8-9-* _____ Time _____ *1:30 p.m.* _____

WHILE YOU WERE OUT

M _____ *Nancy Long, President* _____

of _____ *Chamber of Commerce* _____

Phone (_____) _____ *555-6329* _____

Area Code   Number   Extension

TELEPHONE	X	PLEASE CALL	
CALLED TO SEE YOU		WILL CALL AGAIN	
WANTS TO SEE YOU		URGENT	
RETURNED YOUR CALL			

Message _*Wanted to let you know that Susan Calhoun*_
*won an award last night at the Chamber of*
*Commerce Banquet--*
     *"Outstanding Young Teacher Award."*

_____ *Sharon* _____
Operator

IN-BASKET SIMULATION #13

Hiring A Science Teacher

It is December, and a science teacher must leave on a maternity leave. You have four applicants for the science position.

Two have been non-renewed from previous positions because of weak discipline in the classroom. One has good grades in science courses but has no experience, lacks self-confidence, and has an abrasive personality. The other spent two years substituting in another state and could not find a full-time job. His academic work in science is average.

The position must be filled by the beginning of the second semester (January 10, 199_).

IN-BASKET SIMULATION #14

Help?

One of your teachers, Joan Kaiser, comes to your office to speak privately about another teacher in your school, Ginny Griffin.

It seems that the night before, Joan and Ginny went to a singles party together at the home of another teacher in your school who lives in a neighboring community. Joan admits she had a couple of drinks in the three hours or so they were at the party, but adds that Ginny had several drinks and, therefore, talked loudly at the party, partially undressed herself in front of others (men and women) at the party, and staggered about the house. To stop the embarrassment, Joan said she convinced Ginny they should leave and go home. Reluctantly Ginny agreed to leave with Joan.

On the way to Ginny's apartment, Ginny babbled about her personal life, saying she had never had a sexual relationship with a man, only with other women, and that she would really like to get Joan in bed with her. She said her step-father had sexually abused her while she was in junior high school. Somewhat incoherently, Ginny told Joan that she had never had a close friend and that she wanted Joan to be her close friend. Ginny said she wanted Joan to help her with her drinking problem and to help her find a good man.

Joan tells you that Ginny is in such bad emotional state that it is affecting her teaching. Joan states Ginny gets easily upset with the students and, at times, breaks down in the faculty lounge and cries. Joan adds that she is not capable of offering the type of support that Ginny is asking for and/or needs.

She wants your advice.

IN-BASKET SIMULATION #15

The Spitwads

You have just talked to Mrs. Hamilton over the phone who is very upset because her daughter, Cynthia, has been the target of spitwads in Mrs. Dunn's class. The mother says it is because her daughter is black and the white students do not like her.

Mrs. Hamilton insisted that you punish the students responsible for throwing the spitwads. She will be happy to give you the students' names.

IN-BASKET SIMULATION #16

The Belligerent Student

TO: M. Principal
FROM: Nora Pitts, Assistant Principal
SUBJECT: Janice Randall
DATE: January 26, 199_

Need your help with a student, Janice Randall.

She constantly skips classes, and detention hall has been of no use - she skips detention hall too.

Every time I discuss with her the various class absences, she curses me and blames the teachers for not doing fun things.

Her parents recently divorced - she is living with her mother, but her mother has been of no help to me. She too blames the teachers.

Any ideas?

IN-BASKET SIMULATION #17

Taxpayer Rights Or Abuse?

Feb. 4, 199_

TO: M. Principal

Three students were caught damaging one of the large air conditioning units last week. The damage repair cost $240. Parents of two boys paid their share of $80 each, but the parents of the third boy, Tom Gray, have refused to pay.

I called the father and he said he didn't have to pay it, he has been a taxpayer in the school district for the past 25 years, and that if we pushed it, he would go to the school board and charge us with harassing him.

I do not think I can do much else.

Mac
Head Custodian

IN-BASKET SIMULATION # 18

The Physical History Teachers

While you were walking down the hall, you notice that Miss Clairborne, a history teacher, appears to have a hand print on her face. When you inquire what happened she informs you she was slapped by Mrs. Armbruster, another history teacher, after they got into an argument in the teacher's workroom.

How will you handle the situation?

Child Abuse or Child Shenanigans?

Mrs. Jones. comes to you and is very upset. She informs you that Ray Benson, a student in her class, has told her that he is afraid to take his report card home. He says his father will "beat his butt" because he is receiving an "Unsatisfactory" in behavior.

How will you handle this situation?

IN-BASKET SIMULATION #20

The Out-Of-Control Student

Sue Wells, a girls physical education teacher, enters your office crying hysterically followed by Cassandra Hueg, a large, muscular girl dressed in a physical education uniform, who in turn is followed by Shirley Rush, the other physical education teacher in your school.

You sit Ms. Wells down in a chair and try to calm her. After a few moments, she is able to stop crying and begins the following story.

"As I left my office to enter the locker room, I encountered two girls shouting obscenities at each other and shoving each other around. I hollered at the girls to stop but to no avail. Finally I stepped between them to separate them, again asking them to stop their shouting. I told them to 'shut up' several times, but the girls would not stop."

Finally in desperation, Ms. Wells said she pushed Cassandra aside, and ordered the other girl to go to the office. "As I was telling the other girl to leave the locker room and go to my office, Cassandra jumped on me, grabbed me around the head with a tight headlock, and attempted to push me toward some lockers. I was really scared Cassandra was going to hurt me."

Ms. Rush then speaks up, saying "I could hear loud voices coming from the locker room as I entered my office from the gym. I walked on into the locker room where I saw Cassandra holding on to Ms. Wells' head and pushing her into some lockers. I ran to the scene and shouted at Cassandra to let go of Ms. Wells. But Cassandra would not let go."

Ms. Rush continued, "As I reached the scene, I pushed Cassandra and grabbed her arm which was wrapped around Ms. Wells' neck. In the struggle Ms. Wells got loose, and I then pushed Cassandra against a wall to restrain her. But Cassandra was still fighting and shouting obscenities at both of us, and in her efforts Cassandra managed to momentarily break free of my grasp. However, I used my forearm to push Cassandra against the wall again, but I guess in reaction, Cassandra lunged toward me and with all her strength, bit me on the outer part of my forearm." (Ms. Rush shows you the bite and blood.) "I screamed, and Cassandra let go. Cassandra then ran to the restroom."

Ms. Rush continued by saying that she followed Cassandra into the restroom, told her to come with her, that they were going to the principal's office.

As you are listening to the two teachers describe the situation, you remember that Cassandra is one year behind in school, that her parents are unable to handle her at home, and that on two occasions, the parents refused permission for testing for special education.

During the time the teachers are telling the stories, Cassandra remains standing, head bowed, and showing no emotion. You glance at Cassandra from time to time, but she makes no eye contact with you.

You are going to have to do something with Cassandra and also with the two teachers.

The Big Test

The state in which your school district is located requires assessment tests for all students in grades 3, 5, 9, and 11. These tests are given in the spring of each year and cover the content areas of reading, mathematics, social studies, and science. The last section of the test requires each student to write a theme of approximately 125-250 words, depending upon the grade level. The writing test presents two topics at each grade level from which the students select one to develop his/her theme. Total time to take all parts of the tests is four hours.

It is common practice, in fact it is encouraged by state education department, for teachers to assist students in the preparation for the tests. Teachers often prepare sample test questions for the students. Even sample test materials are prepared and sent home to parents of students in the designated grades so that practice for the tests can be done at home.

Teachers also develop topics for the writing test in the particular grades. Time is spent in class developing outlines, structuring sentences and paragraphs, and teaching and reteaching proper grammar. Students will write several practice themes in the weeks before the actual test date.

Preparation of the students for the tests is very critical to the school. The results of the tests are published in accordance to state law, and the results by grades are compared among the districts across the state. Also the results by grades in each school must be published in a local newspaper.

The test results are also used by the state department of education in the accreditation process. Schools receiving low scores on the tests are subject to receiving monitoring visits from state department personnel.

Consequently competition among districts and among schools in a district is very keen. Teachers also feel the pressure of having their students do well as there is competition among teachers also, although results by teachers are not published for public consumption. In some districts, school principals' jobs are "on-the-line" if the schools do not raise their test scores

The school district receives the test materials from the State Department of Education approximately two weeks before the designated test date. These test materials are then distributed to the respective schools housing the grades to be tested.

Instructions call for the tests to be administered under the supervision of the principal of each school giving the tests, and at the conclusion of the administration of the tests, the principal is to sign an affidavit indicating that strict confidentiality has been maintained in the administration of the tests.

As principal of your school, you have received the boxes containing the tests for the appropriate grade(s) in your school one week before the test date. The boxes are sealed, but in your office, you open the boxes to insure that the proper tests have been sent. Everything checks out okay.

In addition you pull the booklets containing the directions for the administering the tests, and personally give the booklets to the teachers in those grades in which the tests are to be administered. You keep the boxes of tests in your office, and tell the teachers they are to pick up the tests on the morning of the test day. You also tell them that they will be administering the tests and that you as principal will monitor the administration of the tests off-and-on during the test day.

Three days before the test day, you are visited in your office by Ms. Teresa Cardenas, one of the teachers from a grade to be tested, who tells you that a fellow teacher, Ms. Beth Fitzsimmons, told the other teachers one of the topics included on the writing test for their grade. Ms. Fitzsimmons announced that she was going to get her kids ready.

Ms. Cardenas is very upset and wants to know what should be done.

IN-BASKET SIMULATION #22

To Teach Or Not To Teach?

TO: M. Principal
FROM: Dr. Superintendent
SUBJECT: School Board Agenda Item
DATE: April 4, 199_

The School Board is supportive of the idea that principals should be strong instructional leaders of their schools. As a part of the Board's thinking, I have been requested to consider a policy which would require each principal to teach at least one class per semester each year and to specify the implementation details.

As you are aware, the teachers' union initially proposed the idea to the Board. They made the argument that many principals lose touch with what is going on in the classroom, and that for principals to teach a class periodically would help principals better understand the problems teachers face in the classroom.

I am concerned about your time; that is, do you have time to teach a class along with your other responsibilities. On the other hand there could be some benefits to each of you in terms of what is going on in the classrooms. It certainly could be a good public relations program for us in the community.

The Board has also asked me to present the pros and cons of this idea. I need your opinions.

Let's Do Lunch

Tom Washington, representative for Terminal Life Insurance Company, is a duly approved insurance agent by the school board to conduct business with school district employees regarding various life insurance programs offered through the school district. Five companies and their designated agents have been approved by the board.

Upon return from lunch, your secretary gives you the following telephone message:

To _M. Principal_

Date _4-23-9-_   Time _1:30 p.m._

WHILE YOU WERE OUT

M _Tom Washington_

of _Terminal Life Insurance Company_

Phone (____) _555-1200_

TELEPHONE	X	PLEASE CALL	X
CALLED TO SEE YOU		WILL CALL AGAIN	
WANTS TO SEE YOU		URGENT	
	RETURNED YOUR CALL		

Message _Wants to take you to lunch tomorrow to discuss your personal life insurance program. Will be here about 11:30._

Sharon
Operator

137

IN-BASKET SIMULATION #24

The CPS Dilemma

April 23, 199_

Memo to M. Principal:

Mrs. Bortz, PTA President, called this morning. She wants to come in to talk to you about a phone call she received from a mother who claims that the school turned her in to Child Protective Services. It seems that the mother wants Mrs. Bortz to find out how many other parents have been turned into CPS.

Is tomorrow morning OK for you to see Mrs. Bortz?

Martha (Secretary)

IN-BASKET SIMULATION #25

The Shooting

You are in your office working on a report. The phone rings (11:30 am). It is a teacher hysterically calling from the cafeteria saying that a boy has been shot by another boy. She says that the P.E. teacher is trying to help the injured boy, and that the boy with the gun fled the school. She adds that other students in the cafeteria are screaming and crying, and then she hangs up.

IN-BASKET SIMULATION #26

Health Hazard ?

May 5, 199_

Memo to M. Principal:

Mrs. Penn, a records clerk at the local hospital, called to inform you that Mr. Wonderful, the art teacher, has been diagnosed as having AIDS. She says that she saw his health records at the hospital and demands that he be fired immediately. She said she will take this issue to the school board and even the newspaper if she does not receive satisfaction.

You may want to call her back.

Martha (secretary)

IN-BASKET SIMULATION #27

Personal Business or Monkey Business

The school district policy regarding local leave is as follows:

LEAVES AND ABSENCES, EMPLOYEES

Local leave shall be granted contractual employees without loss of pay when absence is cause by personal illness or illness or death in the immediate family as follows:
1. Six days for ten-month employees.
2. Seven days for eleven-month employees.
3. Eight days for twelve-month employees.

The following restrictions shall apply to the use of local leave:
1. A maximum of two days for religious holidays.
2. A maximum of three days may be granted because of the death of a member of the immediate family.
3. A maximum of two days may be used for personal business. Personal business days are defined as those days in which the employee must conduct or transact a business matter during normal working hours. Examples include but are not limited to purchasing or selling a house, the adoption of a child, or the settling of an estate. Personal business leave may not be used on the following days:
   a. The day before or after a holiday.
   b. On an inservice day.
   c. On weather make-up days.
   d. The last week of school.
4. A maximum of one day may be granted for an emergency.

The employee is expected to notify his/her supervisor regarding taking any leave covered under this policy prior to the absences, however, prior approval by the supervisor is not necessary.

Adopted: 199_

Mrs. Joyce Lynn is one of your best teachers. She has chaired several important school committees. She is a team leader, a member of the superintendent's advisory committee, and a very active teacher union member.

One afternoon after school, she catches you in the hallway and says she has a problem. "My daughter is getting married a week from Saturday, and I am going to need some time off to get ready for the wedding. Would it be possible to have Thursday and Friday off before the wedding, and count the days as personal business days?"

You are in a hurry to meet a parent in your office, and you quickly tell her to send you a note regarding her request.

What will your decision be?

IN-BASKET SIMULATION # 28

What's The Matter With Craig?

TO: M. Principal
FROM: Cindy Matson
SUBJECT: Craig Edwards
DATE: May 15, 199_

As you know Craig and I are on the same teaching team with two other teachers. I really do not want to get anyone in trouble, but the other two teachers asked that I as team leader send you a memo regarding Craig's behavior this school year.

In general, Craig has not been cooperative, at times refusing to attend team meetings whereby important planning is taking place for the following week. Also, if he attends the team meetings, he insists he is capable of planning his own activities and that we don't have any good ideas to offer him.

I know that Craig is quite a bit older than the three of us female teachers and that he has many more years experience. But he doesn't have the right to put us down and refuse to work with us. We have tried to be nice to him, and at times, did things his way even if we disagreed with his ideas. He has lost his temper on numerous occasions, sometimes cussing us, and often shouting at us when he became upset with us.

We need your help. We are not sure we can go through another school year with Craig as a team member.

Teacher In A Rut

Reminder to Self:

Think about moving Mrs. McFarland from one grade to another.
1. Taught same grade for 15 years
2. Program - stagnant
3. Morale low among other grade level teachers
4. Parents like Mrs. Mc.
5. Long time resident of the community

Mrs. Mc. works hard, but seems to be doing same thing every year. No new ideas and activities in several years.

IN-BASKET SIMULATION #30

Barbara Shouldn't Be Promoted

June 10, 199_

Memo to M. Principal:

Mrs. Linda Marshall, mother of Barbara, called me this morning to say she is afraid Barbara will not be able to do G-4 work next year. I pulled Barbara's record: she was promoted by Vicki Nelson from G-3 to G-4. Barbara's grades have been below average, and her achievement test scores are approximately one year below grade level.

Mrs. Marshall said Mrs. Nelson just gave Barbara passing grades so she could be promoted, that Barbara really was not doing passing work.

Would you like for me to call Vicki or do anything else?

Martha (secretary)

IN-BASKET SIMULATION #31

The Heat Is On

It is July 5 (Wednesday), 7:00 a.m. Your home phone rings, you answer it. The person on the other end is your school's head custodian, a man with several years experience. He says the school's air conditioner is not working. He does not feel the custodians can continue cleaning the school if the school gets hot.

CASE STUDIES

The last section of this book consists of two case studies: 1) Bryson Elementary School and 2) Sugar Creek High School.

In the first case study, the student is asked to assume the role of a first year assistant principal of Bryson Elementary School. The school is located in a small rural community where the people take great pride in their schools but where the students are scoring well below state averages on state mandated tests.

Sugar Creek High School, on the other hand, is located in a metropolitan area of a large U.S. city. Faced with a changing student population and a changing community, the school has had a high turn-over of administrators. The student will be asked to assume the role of the recently appointed principal of Sugar Creek High School, and to map out several short term and long term strategies for improving the educational program at the school.

CASE STUDY

BRYSON ELEMENTARY SCHOOL

Bryson is a small rural town of approximately 600 residents, located on State Highway 175, about 65 miles southeast of the state capital. The town was named in honor of Captain W.T. Bryson who fought in the Civil War.

Bryson was a small settlement of farmers and tradesmen prior to the Civil War, but with the construction of the railroad through the settlement in 1889, it became an incorporated town known as Bryson in 1891. The coming of the railroad provided new opportunities for farmers, tradesmen, as well as merchants, many who followed the railroad from the state capital.

The town grew very rapidly and soon consisted of a post office, mercantile stores, blacksmith shops, grist mills, lumber yards, and in 1910, its first bank. Also appearing were doctors and druggists. In 1936, the municipal water system was created. In 1954, the first library was opened in a new building. As the community grew, church groups organized and shared the same church building for several years until each could provide its own site. Presently, there are five churches (four Protestant and one Catholic) within the city limits.

Bryson is considered a quiet, peaceful town consisting of many retired people who have either lived in or around Bryson all their lives or have "returned home" after living elsewhere much of their adult lives. As one local citizen said, "You have to be careful who you talk about to your neighbor, they are probably related."

The Bryson Schools

No doubt the greatest source of pride in Bryson is the public school system. Almost all the town's social activities center around school activities, primarily athletics, band, and school programs such as holiday concerts and elementary school PTA programs. Several residents actively participate and attend school functions throughout the year, even those who no longer have children in school. One man

148

whose three children went through Bryson Schools has worked the chains at home football games and worked track meets for 25 years.

The Bryson Schools have one cafeteria on each of the two campuses in the town. The manager of each of the cafeterias is the only paid employee; parents and other patrons volunteer time during the school year to assist the manager in preparing and serving the meals each day to the students. Participation of students in the school lunch program runs higher than 80% on most days.

The patrons of Bryson have been very supportive of a building program during the past 15 years. After approving a bond referendum in 1981, a new high school was built and opened in August 1984. A new football stadium and agriculture shop was opened at the same time.

The following year saw the addition of an eight classroom building to the elementary school for kindergarten and first grade. In 1990, yet another addition was constructed to the elementary school of six new classrooms and office spaces.

The building program currently in progress consists of a new intermediate building housing grades 4-6; a new band hall and practice rooms, science labs, and athletic locker rooms at the high school, a new baseball complex, and a new track at the football field.

For the current school year, the Bryson Schools, encompassing 76 square miles in Henderson County, has an enrollment of 1300 students, prekindergarten through twelfth grade. The school system has additional programs in special education, compensatory education, gifted and talented, and vocational education.

Bryson Elementary

Located on a large wooded campus at the edge of town is Bryson Elementary (Pre K - 6) housing 770 students. The racial composition for the school is as follows:

African American	9%
Hispanic	4%
White	86%

At-risk students, those considered economically disadvantaged, make up 65% of the total student population at the elementary school.

The elementary school has 56 professional staff including one principal, one assistant principal, one counselor, one librarian, two physical education teachers, two music teachers, and one general science teacher. Seven instructional aides are assigned to the school along with the school secretary and an attendance clerk. The school also has a full time nurse assigned.

Classroom teachers are as follows:

Pre K	3
Kdgn	4
G1	7
G2	7
G3	6
G4	6
G5	6
G6	5
Spec Ed	3
Total	47

Average teaching experience for the 47 teachers is 10.3 years in the Bryson Schools and 11.5 overall. Seventeen of the 47 teachers hold master degrees, and all 56 professional staff members are fully certified in their areas of assignment. All personnel assigned to the school are white and most live in Bryson community.

Several other facts are also noted regarding the Bryson Elementary School which impact the instructional program. For instance, the elementary school library has an average of six books per student on the shelf. Very few media materials can be found in the library. Classroom teachers frequently contact the town library or the regional education service center for additional media materials.

The classrooms, even though new, were not wired for extensive computer installation. Only one computer has been placed in the classrooms G4-6. Most teachers have expressed little or no interest in adding computer technology to their classrooms. Mr. Walter Olds, a teacher with over 30 years of teaching experience and a former principal of Bryson Elementary Schools, now serving as the science teacher, has developed an excellent science program using six computers he purchased himself. Mr. Olds works mostly with sixth grade students in this science program.

Observing the classrooms, one finds the teachers using a basal reading series, state adopted textbooks in social studies and mathematics, and few supplemental materials. Lots of paper and pencil activities occupy the students' time.

Teachers seldom group students even in the lower grades for reading. In most classrooms, teachers keep all the students "on the same page of the same book at the same time."

A look at the test scores reveals the following results on state mandated tests:

PERCENT PASSING

	Bryson Students		State Averages	
	Reading	Math	Reading	Math
G4	54%	38%	72%	69%
G5	47%	35%	70%	70%

On a writing test administered only in G6, only 36% scored a passing mark, whereas the state average was 73%.

One person who has become very concerned about the state test results is the principal, Mrs. Janice Estes. Mrs. Estes has received pressure from the central office administration as well as the school board and certain local parents "to do something about the test scores." One area newspaper in comparing test scores of the county schools noted that Bryson Elementary School had the lowest test scores of all county elementary schools. Even the Bryson secondary students were lowest or next to the lowest in all tested areas.

Mrs. Estes is serving her fourth year as principal of Bryson Elementary School after serving as assistant principal at the school. She had been a grade five and grade six teacher for eleven years at Bryson before

151

moving into administration. Mrs. Estes came to Bryson after graduating from the state university to marry her husband, a Bryson farm cooperative manager. The Estes family is a long-time Bryson family, and several family members are leaders in the community, especially in the banking and insurance businesses. One of Mr. Estes' brothers is currently vice president of the school board.

Ms. Marne Helms is the new assistant principal of the elementary schools. Although Mrs. Estes had expressed preference for a third grade teacher to become the assistant principal, she was willing to accept Ms. Helms, who was the choice of both the superintendent and the director of instruction.

Ms. Helms is a Bryson school graduate, having moved back home last year to be near her parents, after divorcing her husband and facing the need to raise two small children.

Ms. Helms taught eight years in an elementary school in a suburban district outside the state capital. She received both her bachelor and master degrees from the state university located in the state capital. Ms. Helms contacted the Director of Instruction, Mrs. Patricia Poteet, a former high school teacher of Ms. Helms, regarding a teaching vacancy in Bryson Elementary School. Mrs. Poteet recommended that Ms. Helms apply instead for the assistant principal position, which had become vacant when the former assistant moved to the secondary school as an assistant principal.

Activity:

At an administrative council meeting chaired by Mrs. Poteet, discussion focused on test results from the state mandated tests. Mrs. Poteet has been given the responsibility by the school superintendent to develop a plan "to raise the test scores in the Bryson schools." Mrs. Poteet also expressed concern about other subject areas within the school's curricula. She emphasized the need to address the total teaching/learning process within the schools, and at the same time, be aware of the importance of the extra curricular and co-curricular program to the community. "The schools are the life blood of the community; without good schools, we will not have a viable and progressive community," was the closing comment by Mrs. Poteet.

On the way back to Bryson Elementary School, Mrs. Estes says to Ms. Helms, "We had better get busy; let's meet in my office tomorrow after school."

Assume that you are Ms. Helms, assistant principal of Bryson Elementary School, what ideas do you have? What can you do? How are you going to approach Mrs. Estes? Is she part of the problem? What changes do you see that are needed in the school? What new programs? New instructional approaches? New materials and equipment? What research can you use to support your ideas for change.

Use the attached worksheet to engage in a task analysis of the problem. Prepare an outline of your ideas and thoughts to be used in the meeting with Mrs. Estes. Be prepared to discuss your role in this school district wide effort "to raise test scores in the Bryson school."

BRYSON ELEMENTARY SCHOOL WORKSHEET

Problem (Statement of the problem or opportunity):

Effects   (Behaviors observed in the school)

Causes   (Factors that are contributing to creating the effects):

Solutions (Strategies and techniques to eliminate the causes and resolve
the problem):

CASE STUDY

SUGAR CREEK HIGH SCHOOL

"Dedicated to Excellence in Education" fills the long paper sign at the front entrance of the 2000 pupil Sugar Creek High School. Students, teachers and staff cannot fail but to see this motto every school day as they enter the building.

Sugar Creek High School is one of four high schools in the Westside Public Schools, a school district of nearly 30,000 enrollment located within the fourth largest metropolitan area of the United States.

Westside has a multitude of histories and traditions. During the 19th century and first half of the 20th century, the area was dominated by agriculture stemming from German settlements along the banks of the Sugar Creek. Since the mid-twentieth century, Westside has been in transition almost continuously from a rural setting to a bedroom suburb to an inner-city neighborhood. Westside has always had a mix of middle class residents of both white and blue collar occupations. Today, Westside is also racially and ethically diverse area with a sizable Asian, Black, and Hispanic populations.

It is impossible to fully understand this nearly 50 year old residential community outside the context of the overall metropolitan environment in which it is part.

Westside's past, present and future is tied to the demographic, employment, and housing market trends of the overall metropolis. Recent changes in these trends are expected to greatly influence the direction Westside follows during the next 20 years of its life-cycle. While the future poses many challenges, Westside has the potential to become one of the metropolitan area's premier inner-city school districts.

Today, Westside is a middle-aged community well within the boundaries of the metropolitan city. The age of the housing stock makes the area relatively old for city neighborhoods, yet only four decades ago it was a new booming suburb at the very edge of the metropolis.

In the 1950's and 1960's, Westside fit the typical profile; mostly residential, primarily a bedroom community to the central city, and quickly annexed by the city once population densities provided a sufficient tax base to support the city services required to be provided. The rapid growth of the metropolitan area, however, quickly changed Westside's relative geographic position. By the mid 70's, Sugar Creek had already become a "close-in" suburb.

The housing developments of the Westside area in the 1950's were middle class, single family residential. Westside was quite typical of new middle class subdivisions of the time. Most homes ranged from 1,500 to 2,500 square feet on suburban lots of 1/5 to 1/2 acre. At the time, the rapid residential development of the area resulted in the creation of one of the city's newest suburban school districts, the Westside Public Schools (WPS). As is often the case with a new suburban school districts, WPS became a magnet for further suburban development, attracting families by its ability to satisfy middle class desires for quality education.

Despite its "distant location," Westside was favored by easy access to work and shopping centers via the Interstate. Much of Westside also offered wooded neighborhood environments that have historically been considered premium properties within the real estate market.

Westside participated in a major way in the metropolitan area apartment boom of the 1970's. There are actually three waves of multi-family buildings: 1968-71;1976-79; and 1981-83. Most of the apartment construction in Westside occurred during the first two waves of construction.

By the end of construction boom in 1983, more than 13,000 apartments units had been built in Westside. As a result, many Westside areas went from almost 100 percent owner-occupied, single family housing to areas in which there were more apartment units than single family units.

The construction of apartment complexes began to alter the

156

demographics of Westside public Schools. Such changes became noticeable by 1980. The expansion of apartment complexes throughout Westside allowed for a significant degree of neighborhood integration in the late 1970's in terms of income, race and ethnicity.

By 1980, 23.3% of the housing stock was rental and 20% of the population was minority. The largest minority population in 1980 was the Hispanic population that constituted 11% of the overall Westside population and as much as 28% in particular census tracts. The Black and Asian populations only accounted for 5.2 and 3.4% of the overall population, and no more than 11 and 7.5 % of any census tract population. Today, the Westside community is 51% white, 37% Hispanic, 8% Black, and 4% Asian.

Another demographic change became evident by 1980. The original population of Westside had aged. In general, the mostly Anglo residents were over 65 years, and yet, over 40 percent of the minority population was under the age of 18. Thus, while the overall population declined in Westside between 1980 and 1990, the population of school age children rose. Because many of these new students used English as a second language, this new migration placed a significant burden upon the WPS.

The new migration also lowered average household income in the Westside area. This decreased the purchasing power within the community and weakened the position of commercial interests in the area. Strip centers began to experience falling income, deferred maintenance, aesthetic deterioration, and declining occupancy.

Westside Public Schools

The Westside Public Schools have long been noted for quality elementary and secondary education. The four Westside high schools have enjoyed a national reputation as being some of the finest high schools in the state and nation. The first superintendent of schools of WPS served 22 years, the second served three, the third served ten years, and the current superintendent, the highest paid in the state, has completed twelve years.

157

Likewise, most of the principals of all the Westside Public Schools have generally served several years in the same school leaving the school only because of being promoted to a central office position or taking state retirement.

The reputation of the WPS has changed somewhat in recent years, however. Largely as a result of its rapidly changing student population, state standardized test scores for elementary, middle, and high schools in the Westside schools are generally lower than other area districts. Westside test results are indicative of the sudden increase in Hispanic school age children in the area, for many of these students speak Spanish as their primary language. Indeed, in many ways the statistics are high for a school district that has only recently had to confront the challenges of teaching non-English speaking youngsters.

Forty percent of all students in Westside Schools are Hispanic. Several elementary schools have Hispanic populations in excess of 50 percent. Because of this population of relatively poor first generation Hispanics, 48 percent of all Westside students are classified as economically disadvantaged and 24 percent are characterized as having limited English proficiency. That latter statistic is about five times greater than other surrounding school districts.

On state tests, only 41 percent of the Hispanic students pass the high school graduation exit exam, whereas 81 percent of the white students pass the exam. White students average 973 on the SAT, Hispanic students average 838.

Sugar Creek High School

Mr. Larry Scott is the principal of Sugar Creek High School. Mr. Scott became the principal as a result of what is referred to by the teachers as the "Thursday Night Shuffle."

Dr. Eric Spencer, Superintendent of Westside Public Schools, on Thursday, January 12 of last year, notified the principal of Sugar Creek High School that she was being transferred to a central office curriculum position. Mr. Scott was called and told he was to move from the principalship of Piney Point Middle School to the principal of

Sugar Creek High School, one assistant principal of Sugar Creek High School was told to transfer to Northside High School, and an assistant principal of Jackson Middle School, Ms. Margaret Wolf, was called and told to report to Sugar Creek High School; all the transfers were to take place immediately.

All were told by Dr. Spencer to clear out their offices on Thursday evening and go to their new assignments by 7:30 a.m. Friday morning. Mr. Scott and Mrs. Wolf joined two other assistant principals at Sugar Creek High School: Mr. Donald Wells and Ms. Andrea Schaffer.

Prior to the "Thursday Night Shuffle", teachers were complaining about the lack of leadership by the principal, Ms. Watson. Parents were going to the school board meetings protesting the lack of strong discipline in the school, and student scores on the state tests were rapidly declining.

One of the assistant superintendents reported to Dr. Spencer that the school was dirty and numerous restroom fixtures were damaged beyond repair. The director of bilingual education program for Westside Public Schools felt the majority of the Sugar Creek High School teachers did not support bilingual education, and that he was having great difficulty finding bilingual teachers who wanted to teach at Sugar Creek.

Dr. Spencer tried to be patient with Ms. Watson, after all she was promoted from assistant principal at Sugar Creek to the principal's position only the previous year. In fact, Sugar Creek High School has had five principals in the last eight years. After listening to all the complaints and concerns, Dr. Spencer then met with the site-based decision making team, called Campus Improvement Team (CIT), at Sugar Creek High School without the principal being present, The ten teacher member of the CIT plus the two parents on the team "unloaded" on Dr. Spencer. No leadership, no support, no discipline, and no expectations was the message!

The next day at 3:30 p.m., Dr. Spencer made the four phone calls and thus the changes were tagged the "Thursday Night Shuffle".

Sugar Creek High School has a current enrollment of 2024; 77.5% are minority students (see fall survey). In 1983, only 20% were minority, but in the last decade, the change in the Hispanic student population has gone from approximately nine percent to nearly 60% while the percentages of Asian and Black students have remained fairly constant between seven to ten percent. In the same time period, the white enrollment has decreased from approximately 80 percent to 22.5%.

Sugar Creek High School has 120 teachers, four counselors as well as four administrators. The ethnic make-up of the teachers is as follows:

White	103
Black	6
Hispanic	0
Other	1

The experience levels of the teachers is as following distribution:

	Total	At Sugar Creek
0 - 5	37	62
6 - 10	16	36
11 - 15	22	15
over 15	45	7

Note that Sugar Creek High School opened 22 years ago.

All of the counselors began as counselors at Sugar Creek High School, and have been counselors for less than five years. Three of the counselors are white, one is Hispanic.

All of the administrators are white, and all except Ms. Schaffer have more than five years experience in administration. Ms. Schaffer is in her second year as an assistant principal at Sugar Creek.

Student Survey

At the end of last school year, one of the teachers in the English Department, while completing requirements for an internship in a school principal preparation program at an area university, under the direction of an university professor and with the permission of the

160

former principal, conducted a student survey. The student survey consisted of 75 questions asking for responses to various topics including personal data (grade level, ethnic background, etc.), classes, tests and homework, teachers, safety, drugs, friends, administrative and support staff, library, food service, discipline, and after-school activities.

The following analyses were reported:

WHAT'S GOOD AT SUGAR CREEK HIGH SCHOOL?

	Category	Student Favorable Responses
1.	Teachers	38%
2.	Computers	36%
3.	Friends	28%
4.	Coaches	28%
5.	Classes, tests, and homework	24%
6.	Extracurricular activities	23%
7.	Library	12%

All other areas received less than ten percent favorable responses from students.

HOW TO MAKE SUGAR CREEK HIGH SCHOOL BETTER!

	Category	Student Response
1.	Lighten up on dress code	52%
2.	Have more extracurricular activities	38%
3.	Make learning fun	37%
4.	Better food in the cafeteria	35%
5.	Explain homework better	23%
6.	Don't be so strict	23%
7.	More time on computers	20%
8.	Have more field trips	15%

All other items received less than ten percent student response.

HOW CAN WE HELP YOU?

	Category	Student response
1.	Help with personal problems	31%
2.	Explain homework/class work better	28%
3.	Understand the student's needs	28%
4.	Help us learn better	26%
5.	Don't be so strict	22%
6.	Listen and talk to us more	16%
7.	Less homework	15%
8.	Have more extracurricular activities	13%
9.	More tutorials	11%
10.	More time between classes	10%

All other areas received less than ten percent student responses.

Activity:

Assume that you are the principal, Larry Scott, of Sugar Creek High School. You have been in this new assignment for just a few weeks. Several questions have been raised by the superintendent in private conversations with you.

1. What are your short term and long term strategies for providing leadership at Sugar Creek High School?
2. What major problems must be addressed, what resources do you need to solve the problems, and what is your time schedule for solving these problems?
3. What major changes do you foresee for the school which will impact the policies, budget and programs at Westside Public Schools?

But you have other questions and deep concerns about the school. You also have several ideas as to what as principal you want to do. Discuss these questions and concerns, and list several of the ideas you have regarding the improvement of Sugar Creek High School.

FALL SURVEY
ETHNIC ENROLLMENT SENIOR HIGH
1983/84 TO 1194/95

SUGAR CREEK HIGH SCHOOL

Year	Asian	Black	Hispanic	White	Total	Minority
1983	118	71	165	1451	1805	19.6%
1984	118	68	150	1271	1608	21.0%
1985	248	164	363	1538	2313	33.5%
1986	273	172	429	1321	2195	39.8%
1987	227	166	459	1069	1922	44.4%
1988	196	179	565	933	1876	50.3%
1989	170	209	681	806	1868	56.9%
1990	193	221	850	774	2040	62.1%
1991	212	194	953	587	1947	69.9%
1992	222	187	1066	536	2011	73.3%
1993	220	205	1152	506	2084	75.7%
1994	196	178	1193	456	2024	77.5%
Total	9.7%	8.8%	58.9%	22.5%